The Tale of a Trooper

The Tale of a Trooper

A Classic Account of the New Zealand Mounted
Rifles During the First World War

Clutha N. Mackenzie

LEONAUR

The Tale of a Trooper
A Classic Account of the New Zealand Mounted Rifles During the First World War
by Clutha N. Mackenzie

First published under the title
The Tale of a Trooper

Leonaur is an imprint of Oakpast Ltd

ISBN: 978-1-78282-950-8 (hardcover)
ISBN: 978-1-78282-951-5 (softcover)

http://www.leonaur.com

Publisher's Notes

Contents

CHAPTER 1
Mac Becomes a Trooper

A winter storm raged across the ridges and tore in violent gusts down the gullies, carrying great squalls of fleecy snow. The wind swept the flakes horizontally through the gap where the station track ran an irregular course through the bush; and, though but a short hour had passed since the ominous mass of black cloud had swept over the early morning sky, the ground was already thickly powdered.

A ramshackle hut stood beside the track where it entered the bush, and in a rough lean-to, where firewood, tools and saddlery were piled more or less indiscriminately, two unkempt station ponies, saddled and bridled, stood in somnolent attitudes. Huddled hens sheltered from the searching blasts, which swept in eddies of snow, ruffling the feathers of the hens and driving the tails of the horses between their legs.

Charley and Mac had come thus far on their way out to have a look at the stock in the big paddocks higher in the hills, before the thickening snow had made purposeless their going further. So, they had dropped in to see old George, the rouseabout, and have a yarn with him, or, if there were no signs of the weather clearing, to consider the question of work in the wool-shed.

"Hullo, boys!" mumbled George. "I reckon as thar' ain't no use us gittin' art jist now. I thinks the fire's the best place ter day. Squat yerself in that thar cheer, Mac, me boy. Jinny! get some tea," he roared hospitably through the wall towards the wee kitchen where his hard-working little wife was making bread for her large family of children who were away at school. "And I'll give yer a toon on the grammephone."

Nothing averse, the two stockmen settled down before the big log fire in George's den, aromatically smoky from firewood and tobacco, with its walls papered from odd paperhangers' samples and prints from Victorian journals, and with domestic odds and ends lying here and there. The good lady speedily produced the tea and added cakes and scones, while George brought into action his cheap American machine and its hoary old records; vague, scratching echoes here in the depths of the bush of the gay sparkling life of Piccadilly and Leicester Square by night, laughing theatre crowds and wonderful women—a life worlds away from George and his rough, but hospitable hearth. He laughed where sometimes there were jokes, more frequently where there were not, and the other two laughed good-naturedly in concert, for the machine scratched so badly that they could not distinguish a word, though George, remembering them in the freshness of their youth, was blind to their growing infirmities. If the two laughed heartily, or expressed in words the good qualities of a record, those, in addition to George's particular cronies, were given a second or a third run.

They grew rather tired of this entertainment, and turned their attention to the domestic bookshelf and the family treasures which adorned the walls and the mantelpiece. In a glass frame was an army biscuit of army hardness on which Mrs. George's brother had written a letter on a distant Christmas Day in South Africa and had posted to her. They deserted other relics for a large book of Boer War pictures, whose leaves they turned together, while the old gramophone ran unfalteringly onwards through its extensive repertoire.

"Those times must have been great," said Charley.

"Don't those chaps look as if they're enjoying themselves?"

"Not half. Cripes! I wish I had been there."

"Why in the devil didn't that bloomin' war come in our time?"

★★★★★★

"Not our luck. You know, Mac, if we'd been the same age we're now, we'd have been there."

Another month passed on that station, and the two stockmen, alone on their beats, rode day after day across the wild ranges and down in the ravines. Along the whole of the east ran a range of mountains, more than a hundred miles of them, their lower slopes clothed in heavy bush, and their serrated summits deep in winter snow. Standing in the north, grand and solitary, was the massive blue-white shape of old Ruapehu, his fires quenched these many years, and, near him, the active cone of Ngaruahoe, whose angry, ominous smoke-clouds rained ashes sometimes on the surrounding country, but more often his wisp of yellowy-white smoke trailed lazily to leeward, or mounted heavenwards in cumulous shape.

Occasionally, on his rounds, Mac dismounted on the summit of a ridge, threw the rein over a stump and settled down for a smoke, his back against a log, his dogs at his feet, a wild ravine below him, then

8

ridge after ridge, bush-topped or strewn with charred trunks and rotting stumps, and, away beyond, the two great snow volcanoes.

They were his friends, and, of all times, he loved most these moments spent in contemplation of those grim reminders of the strength of Nature, of the untamed fires which burnt beneath and of the smallness of man. He revelled in the changing colour tones of the rugged ice cliffs, of the mountain mists and of the rolling deliberate smoke-cloud. Grand, too, was the space of it all, wonderful the air, and here, high on this ridge, human selfishness scarce seemed to be of this world. Sometimes, when he had been out here ready to start mustering at dawn, he had watched the first glow of coming daylight on the summit of Ruapehu, and again, at the end of a long summer day when the smoke of many bush-fires was in the air, he had watched for an hour or more the delicate lilacs, the greens and blues, reds and golds, the shadows deepening beneath the buttresses, and the slow melting of the last warm glow into the cold steely colour of night.

He knew of no happier life than this of his—dodging along most days on his station pony with his dogs following; always on the alert to discover anything amiss with an odd sheep or a cattle-beast; sometimes working with the sheep in the yards, dipping, crutching and such like, or going off on jaunts to neighbouring stations or distant townships. It was a life where there was opportunity for the whole of a man's skill and wit, and where monotony and loneliness were not. After the day's work he and Charley took turns in cooking the dinner, while the other went for the mail. The several-day-old paper lost nothing by its age. The meal finished, they smoked and read the news, had a game of cards, perhaps, with someone who had ridden over, and turned into bunk for sleep that was never sounder.

Thus, dawned the early days of August with Mac and Charley. There had been Balkan rumblings, which, it hardly seemed possible, could echo in these distant hills, but speedily the shadow on Europe darkened, and they rode out to the cross-road to get the mail as soon as the coach arrived. And then, through the long spun-out wire which connected many scattered homesteads with the outer world, came the great news—War with Germany.

Mac and Charley piled up the great logs that night and sat before the glowing timber until five in the morning, talking over the probabilities and the possibilities of the moment. Already the old station life seemed behind them. What mattered it if the sheep got on their backs or the cattle broke their silly necks? And of the future they had a vague apprehension—a terrible sinking that there might not be a military force required from New Zealand, and, if there was one formed, it was scarcely likely to reach Europe before the war was over. That the Dominion would wish to send a force, they never doubted, but whether England would want it was another question.

They drew out their military kits from beneath their bunks, emptied their contents on the floor and investigated them keenly with an increased interest. They donned the tunics. Charley's body was shortly garbed as that of a lieutenant of the West Coast Infantry Regiment, but the rest of his figure was not in keeping with his wild red hair, his bristly jowls awaiting the week-end shave, his open shirt and his rough working trousers. Mac was in the Manawatu Mounted Rifles, but had not risen above the humble, though estimable rank of trooper, and his tunic fell far short of covering his lengthy arms. Between bursts of laughter, they chatted away on these eccentricities, and inspected the rest of the garments with a critical eye, commented on their fitness for the field, and hung them finally on nails in the wall. Regretfully they turned into bunk, and sank into sleep too deep for dreaming.

The next day Mac came across George at work on a break in a fence.

"Good mornin', Mac, me boy. How's things? This 'ere slip do be a fair devil."

"Oh, stock's all right. What d'you think of what's happening?"

"Aw, yer mean this 'ere row in Yourope? It's a bit of a business, ain't it?" George was contemplatively filling his well-seasoned cherry, and spoke of Europe as a sort of detached planet, and of its concerns as far from likely to set going eddies in these wild hills. "I reckon as they'll 'ave a bit of a go. Wot d'you think?"

"I'm off to it, George, by the first bloomin' boat that goes."

"Haw! Haw! Haw!" roared the old boy, throwing his head back, and swaying with the fullness of his mirth. "What an 'ell of a joke." Mac, too, chuckled as he sat in the saddle.

"True, dink, George, I'm going."

"Go on! Yer can't kid me that. Why the bloomin' thing's in Yourope, an' it'll be all over in a couple o' shakes."

"Never mind. I'm off. And so's Charley."

But George was not to be persuaded, and Mac left him still enjoying the joke.

That night a distant voice on the telephone said it was probable that an overseas force would be despatched as soon as possible, and inquired if they would willingly volunteer.

"You bet your boots!" Mac shouted down the line.

"Good," said the voice. "The whole regiment has so far volunteered."

Three or four days passed wearily by, for all interest had gone out of the old life and they were restless for the new. Disturbing rumours came vaguely from without of an overseas force ready and about to sail, and Charley and Mac unanimously decided that they were too far from the centre of things, and that they must proceed closer to civilization without delay. Finishing the day's work, they went through the Saturday overhaul and made themselves presentable in public, saddled the horses, and, in the refreshing spring evening, rode away down the narrow winding road through glades of bush and lonely valleys to the railway line. There they stayed at a neighbouring homestead, gathering round a great, crackling log-fire to talk over the wonderful days ahead.

Early in the morning they were again on the road for a small country town where lived Mac's colonel. Pleasant indeed were those hours, riding ever over the glorious hills and down in the valleys, and as they rode along the world seemed a wonderful place.

The colonel met Mac's anxious inquiries, as to whether there was any chance of his getting away, with a cheery laugh.

"No doubt about it, my boy. You'll be all right."

But he was not able to relieve Charley's anxiety as to what was taking place in infantry regiments. He told them of the advance guard which lay at anchor in Port Nicholson awaiting orders to sail at any moment for an unknown destination, but said it was no use trying to get away with it, as it was composed only of infantry regiments from the cities.

It was well towards midnight when they returned, Mac in absolute peace of mind, but Charley still unsettled. His headquarters were a hundred miles away, and their sport of a host spent the following day running them down in his car, so that Charley might have final satisfaction, and that night, as the car spun homeward hour after hour through the darkness, there was no marring thought in the minds of the two would-be campaigners.

Mac seized two hours' sleep on a sofa, and then crept away into the night to catch a mail train which, rumbling northwards through the hills in the small hours, sometimes stopped near here to water. Late the next afternoon he acquainted his relatives of his intentions, spent a day or two with them, wished them a cheery farewell, and early the next

Sunday, ere the morning mists in the gullies had fled before the first rays, he was again riding up the hill to the old homestead.

He slung his civilian clothes into his tin box, cast his eye rather sorrowfully over his agricultural books as he stowed them away in a kerosene case, and regarded his bare walls whimsically as he removed from them his few precious photos and one or two quaint sketches. He wondered vaguely while he donned his khaki breeches and *puttees* what strange lands he might wander in, what queer beds might be his, and what great adventures he might have ere he would again take that mufti from the tin trunk. And would this fine old station life ever be his again? In the evening he rode to neighbouring homesteads to bid farewell to many whose homes had been his, and whose thoughts would go with him on his unknown travels. Finally, he parted with his dogs.

The next morning, no longer a stockman, but a soldier of the king, he turned his back on the station, a home of pleasant memories, and travelled slowly the long road to the camp. His mare had come straight from a long spell of grass, and it was late in the afternoon of the following day before he dismounted finally in his squadron lines. Here already, in the middle days of August, were several thousand splendid men—a battalion of infantry, a regiment of mounted rifles, a battery of artillery, medical corps, engineers, signallers and service corps; fine men all, accustomed to life in the open, strong of build, active of movement and infinitely amused with everything around—splendid comrades with whom to embark on a campaign.

Mac made his way to his tent, where he was straightway at home with mates of previous camps and station days.

Chapter 2

Mac Embarks for Overseas

Six weeks dragged slowly by. A few days after they came into camp, there were ten great transports ready to take overseas the Expeditionary Force of 8,500 men, horses, guns, limbers and stores, and always there had been orders to be ready for instant embarkation and that the probable date of departure was a week ahead. Constantly that day was put off, and again put off, delay followed delay, while the men speculated on the cause, condemned the authorities and blasphemed generally. The war would be over before they could get anywhere near the front, and they chafed vainly. The troopships lay in the harbours, the men were ready in camp, why not embark?

With the exception of this uneasiness of mind, nothing spoilt the full enjoyment of the spring days. All day the sun shone bright and strong from a blue sky, the warmth tempered by pleasant breezes from the sea or the mountains, and at night the stars stood out brilliantly in the great dome above. Used to many camps in the past, accustomed also to cooking and to battling generally for themselves, they were as much at home as ever they were in the lines of white tents, and for most of them these were lazy holidays after the hard life of the bush and the sheep-runs. The army was generous in its supply of food, and much good butter, jam, meat and bread, which would have been luxuries indeed in the months to come, went to waste in Awapuni incinerators. And day after day came cars from towns and farms and stations within two hundred miles, bringing tuck-box after tuck-box containing the choicest products of the home larders.

The red sun, lifting above the eastern hills, found long irregular lines of horses straggling across dewy fields to water at the rushing streams of the Manawatu River. On one bare-backed horse of every four sat a trooper, clad sketchily in shirt and breeches tugged on hastily, as a sergeant had called the roll. They played the fool as they passed, laughing and chattering, losing their horses in their madness, all making thorough nuisances of themselves and all atune with the fresh glory of the dawn.

Usually, during the day, in independent troops of thirty or forty men, they wandered about the district, among the pleasant suburban homes of Palmerston, along shady country roads or up into the hills. They walked or cantered for an hour or so, and then, selecting a likely-looking homestead, they would unsaddle and unbridle their mounts and leave them to graze the succulent grass at the sides of the road, or roll if they wished, while a man was put at both ends of that stretch of road to prevent their straying. Then the others would lie in the shade or sun themselves on the bank opposite the homestead, sleeping, smoking, reading or playing cards. Scarcely ever did the oracle fail to work. The door of the house would open and a fair maid appear, *anon*, a mother and a sister. The first would come tripping down the path to the soldiers and inquire:

"Mother says would you like some tea?"

"Well," they would reply, "it wouldn't be a bad idea, would it? But, I say, wouldn't it be a lot of trouble?"

"Oh, not at all."

And she would skip away back to the house to the innards of

which, mother and sister, regarding the preamble as a mere formality, had disappeared to get things under way. A brief interval was followed by the appearance of large trays of cups, the whole of the household crockery from the drawing-room, breakfast-room and kitchen, with scones and cakes, and all the luxuries of the storeroom, and, perhaps, apples from the barn. The good family, as is only in keeping with proper hospitality, would join in the feast; and the disappearance of two or three cheery troopers into the house to assist in washing up would end one of those irresponsible, warm-hearted little scenes which were so many in those far-away days of August '14. Another hour or so on the march in the middle afternoon, and they would return to camp, to "stables" and evening.

Palmerston normally was never anything else than a quiet country town of sober habits and eminent respectability, but now the echoing emptiness of her streets was gone, the lights shone brilliantly across the Square, the air was full of the murmur of the crowd, the tread of heavy boots, the tinkling of spurs and glasses and the laughter of merry parties. Perspiring waiters and flustered waitresses fed the hordes in the hotels, while the baths worked overtime. The road to the camp lay like a searchlight beam across the landscape—the cloud of never-resting dust lit by the strong headlights of a thousand taxis which careered along the rough road, careless of life or of their own future. Happy and weary, the men came streaming back to camp, entering by the front if before "Lights Out," through the pine plantations if after.

At length embarkation orders became concrete and remained so.

The camp buzzed with excitement, and, when night came, all were busy getting the gear ready. No one slept, and, in the dark, silent hours before the dawn, the camp was struck. The neat lines of tents became merely small bundles and odd poles, while hundreds of figures passed hither and thither amid blazing fires of straw. In the early light the regiment moved away from the pleasant camp of Awapuni, the first of many such abodes. In the middle of the morning, struggling engines creaked away with the long lines of horse-trucks and carriages of rowdy troopers who cheered wildly as they set out at last upon their adventures.

They crawled along the low country of the Manawatu, then along the rough cliffs above the sea, over the hills, and at length down the rocky gorge to Wellington. The troops detrained, watered and fed the horses, hung about for a while, and eventually led the horses to the wharves. Four great grey transports lay alongside, and the sun shone down hotly on a scene of seething activity, a crowd of troops working with the energy of enthusiasm, long strings of horses filing up huge gangways and disappearing into lines of horse-boxes around the bulwarks, or swinging aloft singly by cranes to be lowered swiftly into the black depths of holds.

Mac led his terrified mare up the steep gangway and down into a hold where he left her with regret. Mac's squadron was to embark on another ship, except some men who were to look after the horses. This transport lay at Lyttelton. So, Mac and his cobbers had a few hours' leave pending the departure of the southward ferry steamer at eight o'clock, and they, in the meantime, went up the town to have a good time and to turn out old friends. They did not waste these few short hours, the streets rang with their enthusiasm, and the departing steamer took away from the pier a singing, rollicking crowd of happy warriors. Mac slept soundly on a table, and awoke in the morning to find the vessel was berthing at Lyttelton.

Disembarking, they filed round the wharves to where two troopships lay opposite each other, and embarked again on H.M.N.Z.T. No. 4, the S.S. *Tahiti*. Mac grabbed what looked about the best bunk in the murky depths of the 'tween decks which was the squadron's allotted space, and wrote his name in several places on the boards. The lucky ones got breakfast during the forenoon, those who were lazy dodged fatigues and slept in out-of-the-way corners in the sun, and so Mac and his cobber Bill might have been found comfortably dozing on a great pile of onions on the aft boat deck.

They found such seclusion most satisfactory on these turbulent days of movement, except for occasional visits to see that no blighted trooper was trying to beat a fellow for his "possie" in the hold. Trains kept rumbling out of the tunnel beneath the great hills, bringing more troops, horses and stores, and all the afternoon the gangways were crowded with these coming on board. By four, embarkation was complete and a throng of people who had massed behind a barrier to see the last of the troops, flooded on to the wharf.

Secrecy had been strictly kept as to the time of departure, and so the public were few to what there might have been. Pretty girls were wildly enthusiastic and were not particular as to how many troopers they fondly took farewell of, women smiled and laughed, though there were often tears in their eyes, and the men were laboriously humorous. A band played airs which the bandmaster considered suitable to the occasion, the troops, swarming on the railings and the rigging,

15

sang lustily snatches of song; and finally, amidst the fortissimo strains of the National Anthem, a wild holloing from every one, and a bellowing of fog-horns, the ships drew slowly away from the wharf. They manoeuvred awkwardly out through the moles, while the throng on shore became but one black shape beneath a sea of fluttering handkerchiefs.

That night the two ships steamed slowly to the north. Mac landed horse-picket, and for four hours he paced a length of the boat-deck up and down past fifty horses' heads, while the wind howled mournfully in the rigging and the ship swayed easily to the swell. Morning broke, with a dull sky, a dull sea and many miserable troopers. Towards midday they were joined by two vessels from the south with the Otago troops, and in the middle of the afternoon the whole four hove to in Cook Strait, awaiting the four transports from Wellington. But contrary orders came, and so, entering Wellington Harbour, they dropped anchor towards evening. A gale came down in gusts from the hills around, bringing furious squalls of rain; and Mac, in heavy oilskins, again paced the boat-deck.

Dawn broke grey and drear, and the troops were in the depths of depression. It was not the ill weather which distressed them, but at the eleventh hour, in the middle of the night, a picket boat had brought unwelcome despatches and now all hope was gone, all faith lost. "Owing to unforeseen circumstances, the transports will not at present sail, and orders for disembarkation will be issued in due course." So ran the death sentence.

Most of the infantry remained on the transports, but the other branches of the service mournfully disembarked and trekked to the few more or less level places amid Wellington's hills, where they pitched camps. The Wellington Mounteds found a home on Trentham racecourse, and passed a fortnight there, riding along the valley roads and manoeuvring over the steep hills. It was not so bad either, for day after day passed with glorious sunshine and cooling breeze, and the city was in reach by a weary train. There was a grand review which no one particularly enjoyed, and Mac least of all, for he had an attack of influenza. All the long day he rode with a dizzy, aching head; and one of Wellington's very own tearing gales, which whirled upwards great clouds of yellow dust, served not at all to cool his heated brow. And when, late at night, he spread out his straw and lay down, the long day seemed to have been a vague, bad dream. But the fever had gone when morning came, which proves that there are more ways than one of curing influenza.

He had cut short the career of the same disease at Awapuni Camp when out on an extensive movement one night near Feilding. His officer had given him a goodly nip of strong Scotch whisky and had advised him to remain at the first bivouac, but Mac thought that influenza was as bad at one place as at another. So, he successfully guarded a road all night, his horse picketed to a fence, and himself in a greatcoat stretched asleep in the middle of the road.

Once again, the bright stars long before dawn looked down upon the bustle of a breaking camp, looked down upon the flaring piles of burning straw, the collapsing tents and the happy laughing throng of busy troopers. Early in the dewy morning they clattered out of the race-course gates and away down the winding road in the valley bottom. Afternoon found them skirting the harbour beneath the great rocky escarpments of Wellington's hills, and from here Mac espied a sight which gladdened his soul and he lost no time in communicating his discovery to Bill and the others. Across a distant neck of land at the far side of the harbour, he had seen the tall tapering masts of two men-of-war, moving rapidly, and two murky streaks of smoke. This looked like business.

In an hour two great cruisers rounded the far point, and the boys welcomed them warmly as a sort of guarantee that there would be no humbug about this embarkation. Again, came the animated scene as they shipped their horses, again a last night to roam streets, which echoed with mirth far into the night, and again the crowded piers aflutter with handkerchiefs, drawing away in the distance. The *Tahiti* passed close astern of the two cruisers, the Japanese *Ibuki* and the British *Minotaur*, and cheered their crews lustily as they came abeam. The whole fleet anchored in the stream. All night long the Morse lamps winked at the mastheads, the ships' lights twinkled on the water in long twisting lines, and the great glow of a million lamps of the city lit with fire the waters of the harbour, and the huge hills stood out black against the sky.

A day of squalls followed, and dragged slowly by. Why were the anchors not weighed? Pessimists said they might never leave, and all eagerly watched the warships for any signs of going to sea—an increasing volume of smoke from the funnels, activity on the bridge or more than an ordinary display of signal flags. But there was nothing to bring lasting satisfaction and the grey day ended with a colourless sunset. Towards midnight a tender bumped alongside, men shouted in the dark and packages were dropped with thuds upon the deck above.

Chapter 3

Sorrows and Joys in a Troopship

Mac dragged himself regretfully out of his bunk when a mournful "reveille" had finished echoing along the decks, and went above to see what might be doing. They were off, or, at least, they soon would be. Already the cruisers were coming steadily down the harbour, some transports had weighed, and were awkwardly pulling their heads round to seaward, others sent clouds of steam rumbling in a deafening roar from their safety-valves. The cruisers passed, and each transport followed in her appointed place.

Everyone neglected the work of the moment in that hour of putting to sea, and Mac, perched high on the roof of the wireless cabin, watched it with as much pride and rapture as might an emperor reviewing the grandest of fleets. In single line-ahead, the fourteen great grey ships, their smoke trailing away over the port quarter before a fresh wind, passed down the wild rocky gap of the entrance. The grey seas rolled in a long swell, grey, flying clouds hid the eastern mountain tops. The passengers of an inbound steamer had hurried on deck, clad lightly against the chill wind, sent a faint cheer to each passing ship.

Hundreds of people waved vigorously from the western shore, having come far to see the last of the adventurers, and the garrisons of the forts looked like silhouetted maniacs above the fortress mounds. They, too, faded in the distance, and at length the reefs with their white surge, and Pencarrow Light high on the cliffs above the poor rusty remnants of a wreck, were far astern. The leading vessels had lifted their bows westward through the Strait, and each following ship was in turn changing course. At sea at last, Mac left his perch, and departed below to his work, a shower-bath and breakfast.

Later in the morning the weather cleared, the cliffs, the hills and the snowy mountains were glorious in the sunshine, and the troops basked at full length on deck while distant points took form far ahead, came on the beam and passed astern. Once through the Strait, the fleet took up its regular formation, the ten transports in two lines of five, with the two large cruisers ahead and the two small ones astern. Late at night, the Farewell Light passed into the blackness, and when dawn broke again, grey, chill and wet, no land was visible behind the reeling stern.

For five or six days—Mac lost count—the transports rolled and creaked and swayed up the grey, lumpy swell, lurched over the crests and plunged away down into the troughs. The spray lifted over the bows and swept along the decks, the wind howled dismally through the rigging, and the ship was wet and comfortless. All was grey—the ships, the sky, the sea and the long trails of smoke fleeing away to leeward. Mac had found a good job on board, together with Joe of the Canterbury Squadron and Jock of his own squadron, in charge of the fodder. Both were from the sheep country and real fine fellows, though Joe had had a college education, while Jock claimed only to have been dragged up in the bush. Three times a day, about an hour before their own meals, they weighed out for the horses the rations of chaff, oats, hay, linseed and so forth, and issued them to fatigues from the troops, the service corps and the mounted machine-gunners, who came slipping and sliding along the deck in heavy gumboots.

The second-class dining saloon of peace days had descended to becoming a fodder room for the horses, and outside its door gathered the boys clamouring for their loads, laughing and swearing and generally hindering Mac and his cobbers at their work. Everything had gone like clockwork in port, but, for the first few days at sea, these practical sons of the bush and the sheep-stations were for the moment put out of their stride. Hefty men lay huddled helplessly on their bunks and others moped about searching for the drier, warmer corners. But the horses had to be fed, though many of them, too, hung their heads in the deepest dejection. The men who were not seasick turned to with a will, and many who were went to work with bold hearts, though feeling too utterly miserable for description when down below on the stuffy, reeling horse-decks.

Mac, in the foolishness of his abandonment, had flung himself at the first spasm of seasickness on to the top of some of his bales of hay; the sweet fragrance of the hay aggravated the evil effects of the rolling, and three days passed like an interminable nightmare. Sometimes the bales and bags slid about the place with the rolling of the ship, occasionally he made weak though desperate attempts to help Joe and Jock who struggled on nobly; but eventually Mac managed to drag himself and two blankets to the top of the horse-boxes high on the boat-deck. There lay rows of men like corpses in their blankets, with pinched white faces peeping out, which smiled pathetically with the bashfulness of returning spirits.

All were on their feet again by dawn of the sixth day, and in odd moments between work peered over the side to catch a glimpse of the low dim line of the Tasmanian coast. They kept along the land for a few hours, and then, forming single line-ahead, steamed slowly up the beautiful sunny waters of the Derwent, with white curving beaches and bush-clad hills on either side. Five ships berthed at once for fresh water. In the afternoon the troops were marched through the town, and the people cheered heartily and hurried in great excitement to see them, bringing cake and fruit and beer.

Some of the boys, keen on adventure, slipped quietly out of the ranks and down side streets, and in the evening other hard cases garbed themselves as stokers, walked boldly past the guard and spent the merriest of evenings in Hobart, to return, perhaps, to a term of C.B. which the holiday was well worth. The other five vessels watered in the morning, and by evening the fleet was again at sea, steaming slowly southwards in a fog towards the southern point of Tasmania. In Morse code each ship in turn mournfully wailed her number, and endeavoured to keep station in the thick pall.

For day after day they swung over the long seas which always sweep across the Australian Bight, but the troops ran about the ships as if they had never been anywhere else, and the horses stamped and whinnied unanimously when the boys stood ready to feed, and looked eagerly for more than the martinet of a vet would allow.

The vet was a brusque man whose job was to look after the horses and not to concern himself with the fine points of military lore, distinctions of rank, or the airs of those officers who thought themselves not made of ordinary clay. He was impatient with people who were incompetent or who hindered him in his work. So, on the occasions when Captain O'Grady violated the sanctity of the fodder-room by stowing there some of his infantry equipment, the Vet would angrily demand:

"Mac! What's that blanky stuff doing there? Is that some more of O'Grady's blanky rubbish?"

"Yes. He said you said he——"

"I don't care a blank what he said. Heave his blanky stuff out of here. O'Grady and his blanky stuff can go to hell. Next time he tries to bring his rubbish in here you tell him to get to blanky blazes with it! See?"

"Righto! I'll do that."

Mac was not soaked in military etiquette, but he rather hesitated, when the captain-quartermaster brought some gear to stow, to instruct him to go to blanky hell with his blanky, etc., etc. However, as soon as Captain O'Grady had disappeared, he and Joe shoved his gear out on the wet deck and the quartermaster constantly finding it there decided to seek other havens.

"I'll teach that blanky infantryman to stow his blanky stuff here," rumbled the vet with satisfaction when there were no more signs of alien goods lumbering the fodder-room.

The first burial of a member of the force took place one stormy day in the Australian Bight. He had died the night before on the *Ruapehu*. In the middle of the afternoon the whole fleet lay to for ten minutes, the troops standing to attention on every ship. The vessels rolled heavily to the rushing silent seas, the troops with grim faces swayed in their long lines on the careening decks. There was no colour to the scene but grey. The greyness, the vast space, the haunting notes of the "Last Post" echoing along the troop-decks, the lonely body deserted on the wide sea, left a deep impression on those light-hearted adventurers. Death! And to be buried here in a lonely ocean grave! Mac wondered how many of these 8,500 men would see New Zealand's shores again, and how many would lie in foreign lands. But such speculations did not trouble him for long. "Carry On" sounded briskly, and Mac returned to his work in the fodder-room.

Like many others of that light-hearted crew, Mac had really not embarked upon these adventures on account of the "ruthless violation of the rights of small nations," with the desire "to crush once and for all the Prussian military despotism," and so forth. Had he given the question deep thought he might possibly have welcomed these reasons as additional charms; though the fact was that he had never worried much concerning why he had come. War, bloody war, romantic, glorious war raging in the Old World, and he obeyed the irresistible desire to join in it.

The whole atmosphere of the life appealed to him, the uncertainty of the future, the unknown destination, the company of all the boys, and the free, fresh life.

More than a week passed and then one morning against the pale blue of the dawn sky showed low dim outlines of deeper blue, and towards midday the fleet entered the wide waters of King George's Sound and cast anchor with the *Tahiti* nearest the sea. On the upper reaches of the Sound lay a great fleet of thirty or forty large vessels— the Australian fleet. Mac had not previously known that they were to fall in with them here. For four days they lay at anchor swinging to the tide, in the entrance, lonely and unvisited, while the eager, barefooted, bare-legged and bare-chested men gazed longingly at the distant port and tried to persuade themselves that the vessel must go up there for coal and water.

Several times the life-boat crews lowered the boats and raced clumsily with each other; and once the troops polished and cleaned all the morning for an inspection by the G.O.C. which never came off. Otherwise they drilled at odd times, groomed, fed and exercised the horses and basked in the sun. Rumours were unusually active, and the question of destination was fiercely argued—South-West Africa, India for garrison duty, or France by the Cape or Suez. The course the fleet set after leaving the Sound would partly decide the question.

The first daylight of Sunday, November 1st—a dawn of rare perfection, with the spacious Sound unruffled by any stray breeze, the wide blue heaven unbroken by any cloud—saw that purposeful activity among the ships which immediately precedes putting to sea. Smoke drifted upwards from many funnels, some ships were busy clearing their anchors, while others manoeuvred out of tight corners. First came the men-o'-war, sweeping majestically past the *Tahiti* and out to sea.

Then, in single-line-ahead, followed the transports in grand procession past the *Tahiti's* bows, whose troops stood on the topmost perches to miss nothing of the glorious review. Everywhere to the upperworks of each passing vessel clung the Australians. As each vessel came abreast, wild, enraptured cheering broke out, and, with all the power of healthy lungs, with enthusiasm unreserved, with cooees and *hakas* and scrappy messages semaphored by the arms, the Australians and New Zealanders met in a deep friendship which was to last through years of campaigning and privation.

CHAPTER 4
Lazy Shipboard Life

The *Tahiti* fell in astern of the long line whose foremost ships were almost hull down, and left the Sound empty and deserted. When all were at sea, they took station, the thirty Australian ships in three lines ahead, with the ten New Zealand transports in two lines astern, their leading ships stationed between the three rearmost vessels of the Australian line. The men-o'-war took up positions far ahead on the horizon and on the flanks. Towards evening a nor'-west course was set, which the troops generally accepted as sufficient evidence that Colombo would be the next port of call.

For some days the fleet swung heavily to a considerable swell from the west; and Mac watched, from the boat deck, the long line of careering masts ahead, sliding about like so many drunken matches, spray flying from the bows, and the foaming wake seething from the labouring screws of the ship ahead. It amused him to cast his eyes aft along the boat deck, the full length of which stretched two lines of horse-boxes facing outwards.

With an even keel only the noses of the horses showed beyond the stalls; but, when the vessel rolled heavily to a beam swell, their heads swung in and out like the cuckoos of cuckoo clocks. One moment, as the ship lay well over into a trough, Mac could see nothing but a long line of posts; the next, as she lifted to a sea, outshot those eighty heads. They trod backwards and forwards in regular step, and were cursed constantly by the men whose bunks were immediately below the trampling hoofs. The horses settled down to the life in a wonderful fashion, and through the splendid attention of the troops appeared not a whit the worse for the first three weeks at sea. With the increasing heat and the lack of exercise some of them were growing a little short-tempered; and men, passing along the front of a line of boxes, had to be prepared for a horse occasionally making a grab at him.

Least of all to appreciate the presence of horses in the vessels were the officers of the ships accustomed to Royal Mails and jolly passengers. They now appeared in all the immaculate glory of white ducks; and it almost gave Mac the impression that the horses had taken a special dislike to them. Either they would frequently be bitten at, or else when one of them was standing comfortably on deck smoking, a horse would give a violent sneeze behind him, and he would disappear into his cabin, muttering wrathfully as he changed into a clean suit. And the captain himself was no more pleased when he noticed the way in which the constant trampling of the horses was wearing ugly tracks in his best teak decks.

Every morning and afternoon, when the vessels were not rolling too heavily, long strips of cocoa-nut matting were laid round the boat deck and the length of the upper deck; and the horses were led round and round for a little, though valuable, exercise. Men spread awnings from the front of the boxes, and watered them steadily from above, so that the horses might be as cool as possible. All of this was hard, hot work, to which the men stuck splendidly. Mac, however, had none of it, for, his turn in the fodder-room being over, he was sent to the bridge as a signaller. He knew little about the work, but another signaller was wanted, and he was sent to learn.

It was the best of work, clean, cool and interesting. He did his watches on the bridge, looking down on everything from that exalted position, swept the fleet constantly with his glasses, and did what was told him. He peered into the log book, and closely examined the charts in spare moments when the officer of the watch was not noticing. He examined everything that was to be examined, instruments, code books and distant ships, and altogether thoroughly approved of being a signaller. Often there was work to be done, in daylight by semaphore arms, or international flag code; and at night by Morse lamps, carefully shaded. Mac fumbled about and fell over himself at times before he mastered the mysteries of flag signals—the knots, the halyards and the nautical language.

"AJP tackline J," the skipper would roar; and two of the signallers would fall over each other in a hurried attempt to get it all tied together. And something usually went wrong—the tackline missed out, two J's put on by mistake, or an M instead of a J. Once Mac failed to make fast the two ends, and one hoist of flags went trailing out over the beam. He let them down into the water, so that the weight might swing them inboard, while the other signaller struggled manfully with a hay-rake to grapple them; and the captain cursed and Mac flushed all over, knowing that every ship in the fleet was grinning at them.

Two days out from King George's Sound the fleet was joined by two more transports with Australian troops from Fremantle. A week later H.M.S. *Minotaur* passed down the lines between the ships, and soon after disappeared over the eastern horizon. The fleet had been sailing with carefully screened lights, and now precautions were to be doubled, no dynamos to be run, and navigation lights to be further dulled by several thicknesses of signal flags across the glass. Various small happenings left the troops with a sort of impression that there might be something in the wind.

When, therefore, early one tropic morning the three remaining men-o'-war moved nervously from their stations, rolled great black-brown coils of smoke from their funnels, and nosed suspiciously out towards the western horizon, like three dogs seeking a scent, it was evident the day would not be without interest. Within a few minutes H.M.A.S. *Sydney* set a definite course, and with a foaming wake and a trail of heavy smoke, went off at full speed to the sou'-west. Mac went below for breakfast in the steamy saloon. Word went round that the *Emden* was at the bottom of the business; and men gathered in groups, talking with animation, and gazing occasionally towards the south-west. Later in the morning the Japanese cruiser went off in that direction, leaving only H.M.A.S. *Melbourne* with the fleet.

At about eleven the great news came; and great enthusiasm welcomed it. In the *Tahiti* it leaked out before it was officially announced; and the poor signallers were blamed in consequence. At any rate it was true. About ten thirty the *Sydney* had reported the *Emden* beached and blazing; and that she had gone off in pursuit of another vessel. The *Maunganui* had offered to take the *Sydney's* wounded; but she replied that there were only twelve casualties, sent her thanks, and said there was no need. That was all the troops heard of the fight for some days, though later the *Empress of Russia* passed on her way to pick up the many wounded from the wrecked *Emden*. (See *The Kaiser's Raider!* by Hellmuth von Mücke containing both is accounts, *The Emden* and *The Ayesha*; Leonaur, 2012.)

Then came the crossing of the Line; and in all ships Father Neptunes were busy lathering, dosing and abusing unlucky troops who tried to escape their gentle hands. Crowds of men splashed rowdily about in great sails of water. But a medical officer unfortunately lost his life over these proceedings, and a momentary sadness settled over the fleet.

The New Zealand section went ahead of the main fleet a day or two before reaching Colombo in order to proceed with coaling and watering. Early on a Sunday morning the mist-covered hills of Ceylon took form on the starboard bow; and, later on, a palm-grown shore and natives in catamarans. Then the house-tops, the breakwater and the shipping of Colombo emerged from the luxurious forest and curving shores. About the middle of the forenoon the New Zealand vessels in two lines of five were about to enter the harbour, when the *Sydney* and the *Empress of Russia* were signalled coming up astern; and the New Zealand ships lay to to give way to the men-o'-war. In deep, impressive silence, they passed down between the lines, while the bluejackets and the troops stood at rigid attention, salute after salute sounded from each ship in turn, and ensigns dipped.

Two days at Colombo passed merrily enough with forty-five shipfuls of light-hearted troops exploring that Oriental city for the first time; and at the end of it the Cingalees were left in a dazed condition. Bazaars, wine-shops, native quarters and Galle Face all rang with the delighted shouts of irresponsible troops making the best of a short time; and rickshaws were raced against each other with great effect. Before many hours had passed the Staff announced their disapproval of such unmilitary conduct, and stopped leave; but the men were not overawed by the thunder of the heads, and those who could swarmed ashore from the ships, leave or no leave. At length the vessels went to the outer anchorage, at a safe distance from Oriental seductions. Next morning a tug brought from the shore a washed-out collection of adventurers, and distributed them to their ships.

Under way again, the fleet steered a west-nor'-westerly course for Aden, and the men, none the worse for a little joy in Colombo, settled again to ship routine. Six German sailors from the *Emden* had been placed on board the *Tahiti* at Colombo; and from them Mac heard something of the battle—how the *Sydney* had surprised them when they had some boats' crews away destroying the wireless and cable stations at Cocos Islands; how the *Emden* had been beached and raked by the *Sydney's* terrible broadsides; and the sufferings of the wounded before they were taken off. Mac was interested to notice through the dome of the officers' dining saloon, which projected through the bridge deck, that a German naval officer prisoner drank the king's health along with the rest of the mess.

Several days dragged drowsily by in sweet procession.

Mac was doing the afternoon watch. Between noon and one o'clock the signallers were usually fairly busy while latitudes and longitudes were hoisted and the staff disposed of the last of the morning's work. Then peace reigned for three hours, while the fleet dozed through the hot afternoon, and Mac could see through his glasses lazy figures stretched in deck-chairs beneath shady awnings. He leaned over the starboard light, neglected his lookout, and gazed far down at the swishing water which ran the ship's length at a lazy ten knots. The fathomless blue of the midday sea, with the white marblings from the bow wave, never ceased to draw Mac's gaze. Down in its depths the red jelly-fish went sailing past, and from there, too, came the terrified flying-fish, which went winging away out to the beam, glittering in the bright sun.

The rumbling of the ship's engines filled the air with a sleepy monotone; and Mac was hard put to keep awake. From his cool perch he looked down on snowy awnings stretching fore and aft, though here and there through openings he caught glimpses of mens' bare bodies as they lay sleeping on deck, and of horses' heads hanging low with half-closed eyes. The other signaller on duty was buried behind the flag-locker, probably intending that it should be thought that he was busy putting away the flags used in the last hoists, though that might have been finished a full hour ago. The officer of the watch took an occasional turn the length of the bridge, and now and then rang down to the engine-room for one more or one less revolution per minute; while the quartermaster periodically put the wheel a few spokes this way or that to keep the ship in station with the vessel ahead.

Mac had certainly drifted away to places other than the bridge of a ship in the Indian Ocean, when he was speedily brought back to the present by a vigorous poke in his ribs. He turned hurriedly; and the officer of the watch with perfect clearness conveyed to him by a jerk of his thumb, and a quizzical expression, that the flagship was making a general signal. Mac shoved up the answering pennant, roused the other drowsy signaller, and elicited the information that the New Zealand ships would anchor 1½ miles S.S.E. of Ras Marshag at 17.50.

Mac looked ahead and saw the jagged blue outline of land above the horizon. Towards four o'clock the heads awoke from their *siestas*, and the signallers were kept busy. The forms on the decks below also commenced to stir, whistles sounded, and soon hoses and brooms were busy cleaning the horse-boxes. Half-naked men were at work with brushes and combs in the narrow spaces between the animals; and others poured cooling streams of water about their legs. Feeding time came with an excited whinnying, snorting and trampling, while the men stood along the deck in front with a long line of feed boxes. Then there was a whistle and a chorus of neighing. The men went forward and attached the boxes. Comparative silence followed, while the horses in deep content poked their muzzles down into the feed and blew showers of chaff into the air. For a time, the satisfied munching went on quietly; but at length the horses which had finished first stamped their feet, and tugged at their halter chains, in attempts to get at their neighbours' feeds.

Mac finished his watch, and went below for a salt shower, and after that the evening meal, which was never much to boast about. He went up to the bridge again to investigate Aden from the best standpoint. The evening lights were colouring splendidly the rocky heights of the range above the port. The anchored fleet spread far across the bay, the *Tahiti* being close to the desert shore several miles from the port. It was an evening of perfect calm. The last glow faded from the topmost pinnacles, the stars came out with the brightness of the desert, Morse signals winked from the mastheads, and the mooring lights cast reflections on the calm water. For a time, Mac joined a four for a rubber or so in the cool night air, and then, collecting his blankets from below, went away forward to sleep on top of the horse-boxes with nothing but stars overhead.

In the early morning, before the fresh charm of the desert dawn had fled before the tropic day, the fleet weighed anchor, and, with a great deal of signalling and manoeuvring, took steaming station again. Soon after midday Perim lay on the starboard, its desolate sands shimmering in the noon sun, shortly to disappear astern, veiled by the trailing smoke. It took the fleet five days to steam the length of the Red Sea; good days too, with cooling northerly breezes to air the stuffy horse decks, though the chill nights made the signallers shiver on watch. But the day before they were due at Suez, the whole peaceful running of things was upset by wild rumours, and then by definite fact.

In late weeks it had been generally accepted by everyone that England would be the destination of the Expeditionary Force, and they had settled comfortably to that point of view, and to the prospect of having nothing to worry them for three or four more weeks. Turkey, however, had declared war; and now, they heard, they were disembarking immediately in Egypt. The troops were undecided whether or not to be pleased. Most of them had hoped to see the Old Country and their relatives there. Mac did not care a straw, for he saw no delights in an English winter camp, and Egypt was said to be a fine interesting country. Everyone set about telling wild tales of Egypt; and proceeded to walk more rapidly about the ship, collecting and putting in order shore-going clothes—so that the quiet shipboard life was at an end.

In the voyaging days of 1914, the New Zealand troops regarded their chances of actually joining in the campaign as being regrettably small. It was clear, they thought in their out-of-the-world way, that the enemy would be speedily overrun; that the New Zealand troops were only untrained, untried colonials; that they could therefore expect no more than garrison duty; and that every available Imperial soldier would be thrown into the field before the colonial troops were drawn upon. Consequently, there was an uneasy feeling abroad that, should they once land in Egypt, they would be left there for the duration of the war.

The New Zealand transports, which had taken the lead, cast anchor in Suez bay just as the sun was rising over the desert; and Mac gazed appreciatively at the sweeping bay, the palms, the flat-topped houses, and the open desert, clear cut in the early light. Suez was not adapted for the disembarkation of large numbers of men and horses, and Alexandria was the only harbour with sufficient accommodation. In the early afternoon the *Tahiti* entered the Canal; and there were no dull moments for the next twelve hours. They were surprised to find, at frequent intervals along the Canal bank, strongly wired entrenchments occupied by Indian troops, with whom they exchanged cheers as they passed. At night a moon lit the silent desert in greater beauty; and Mac slept not a wink as the ship slid quietly past mile after mile of the queer waterway. At three in the morning, with a clatter of chains and a good deal of shouting, they moored in Port Said harbour.

Again, there was a day full of interest—bartering with natives, watching the *coolies* coaling, cheering Australian transports as they entered the basin, and examining the mixture of shipping in the port.

CHAPTER 5

Ashore Again

Late in the same afternoon the New Zealand ships put to sea, under orders to steam individually at slow speed to meet off Alexandria at dawn. There was not a great deal of settled sleep that night, for all men were busy packing kit-bags and putting in order shore-going clothes. The days of decks, bare feet and semi-nakedness were at an end, and tomorrow would start again the life of boots and *puttees*, saddles and tents. Men stood in small groups along the deck, shown only by the embers of pipes and the occasional glow of a match.

They watched the low line of the Egyptian shore, deep black against a sky which seemed vaster than usual and more brilliant with stars, and were exhilarated by the knowledge that they would disembark tomorrow in that queer old country. The mess room was filled for a while with a cheery, laughing crowd to hear words of warning from an old soldier concerning the joys and sorrows of Cairo and a few general instructions on life in Egypt.

The ships stood in towards the entrance to the port just as the rising sun gilded the houses and minarets of Alexandria. Soon the gangway was dropped for a pilot to come abroad, and shortly with much chattering that gentleman appeared on the bridge. The captain gazed on the apparition with horror, and the signallers, in security behind the flag locket, were convulsed with mirth. A pale, underfed little Hebrew, not, apparently, the cleanest specimen of its race, clad in something like a dressing-gown and a pair of bath slippers, and topped off by a red *tarboosh* tilted well back and continuing the contour of its nose, it looked about as capable of piloting a ship as a waste-paper-basket. It chattered away cheerfully to everyone on the bridge in a strange lingo, waved its hands alternately here, there and everywhere, and faced in all directions in the attitudes of ancient mural figures. It was serenely unheeding of the business in hand, of the fact that four ships, occupying the narrow fairway ahead, were slowing down, and that three others were coming rapidly up behind, promising trouble.

The skipper recovered from his astonishment.

"Which way?" he said, interrupting a friendly jabber to the third officer.

The figure raised its eyebrows, bared its rabbit teeth and, wildly waving its arms, poured a stream of unintelligible jargon in the skipper's direction.

"Shall I stop her?" yelled the skipper.

A wide, inclusive sweep of the arms was the only reply and the jabbering increased.

"To starboard—or port?" inquired the captain, indicating each with his arm.

To both queries the figure energetically nodded assent.

The captain flushed with anger. The figure looked crestfallen.

Meanwhile the bows were getting dangerously near the stern of the vessel ahead, while the ship astern was overlapping the port quarter. Moles threatened destruction on either beam, and quantities of small Greek sailing vessels were in imminent danger.

The captain seized the little fellow by the shoulder and shook him.

"Damn it, man!" he shouted. "What in hell——!"

The woebegone figure spread his hands in innocent protestation. Then the light of a bright idea suffused his countenance. He went to one side and craned over the rail, gazing first forward and then aft. He did the same on the other side. He repeated the action on both sides. Then a wild yell announced a discovery, and, following his gaze, Mac saw a launch which had appeared from behind one of the vessels ahead. Shrill shrieks from the figure at length drew its attention and a *fortissimo* of jabbering and arm-waving welcomed its nearer approach. A more business-like person came aboard, who took the vessel in charge, the while its late pilot muttered unhappily in the background.

The rest of the manoeuvres went smoothly enough. The only particular incident which amused Mac was watching a trio of Greek sailors tormenting a terrified Egyptian by holding him by the legs upside down over a ship's side, as if intending to drop him into the water.

It was not Mac's luck to disembark immediately on berthing, for his squadron were detailed to clean up the ship after all the men and horses had gone ashore. They stripped themselves of their shore kit, and with hoses and brooms scrubbed decks for hour after hour. In the afternoon Mac did a watch by himself on the bridge for any signals which might be sent. Few came, and it was a sad and lonely bridge deserted after what seemed years at sea. The evening brought unloading of the holds and by the light of great arc lamps stores of all sorts were piled high. It was past midnight before the winches were silent.

Before four in the morning the few remaining troops were again astir, and by daybreak were all on the quay with their equipment. The ship on which were the squadron's horses lay about two miles away, and they set out for her. Mac was very sick, probably for unwisely sampling Turkish delight sold him yesterday by an Egyptian at the ship's side. Unaccustomed boots, a cobbled street and a heavy load did not add to the pleasures of the march. They reached the other quay, and shivered for two hours in the chilly Mediterranean breeze until they were sent on board to unload stores.

Hard work set Mac to rights, and the piles of oats, chaff and hay grew steadily as the forenoon advanced. They scratched up a meal in the depths of the ship, worked again, and then, in the middle of the afternoon, unshipped the horses. One by one they led them up the gangways from the holds, and then, sliding and slipping on their weak legs, down a steep gangway to the low quay.

Once on firm ground, the horses threw up their heels, bucked and neighed in sheer delight. But they overestimated their strength and came sprawling to earth and soon, for lack of breath, quieted down. The squadron led its horses to a piece of waste sandy ground, removed their covers, and let them roll to their hearts' content. They were in excellent condition after so long a voyage in warm seas, and Mac was grateful to the fellows who had looked after them. His had been a pleasure voyage, but they had had no such luck. From 5 a.m. till 9 p.m. it had been groom, clean decks, feed, water and exercise; and then, more often than not, it was horse-picket for part of the night. The temperature of the horse-holes had for a long space never fallen below 110° F.; and five horses had been each man's charge.

★★★★★★

"Where are we going, d'you know, Bill?" asked Mac.

"Sure, I don't know. Some fellers say it's Cairo. Others say it's a place called Zeitoun, and God only knows where that is. Anyhow I hope it's Cairo. Cobber of mine, who'd bin there, told me it was just a bit of all right. Said it was a reg'lar hot shop."

"No such luck, Bill," chipped in Jock. "You don't find the heads sending us anywhere decent like that. Afraid of givin' us too good a time."

"Yes. And the dear old wowser boys at home in N.Z. would get up on their hind legs an' say, 'Is it right that our dear boys should be let go free in such a dreadful city, what with the awful drink, and gamblin' and worse than that, dear brethren. No, we will petition the Minister of Defence to stop the dwedful catastrophe, to put the pubs outer bounds, an' ter never have any wet canteens in the camps. Oh, our poor innocent boys!'"

"Ha! Ha! Ha!" laughed Mac. "Anyway, it'll be a bit of a change. Wonder how long we'll be here?"

"Gawd only knows," answered Bill. "Mare looks well, Mac. Legs a bit puffed, that's all."

They wandered off in due course to water and feed. They rugged the horses, and at six o'clock entrained them, packing them tightly in the trucks. The men had a bit of a meal then themselves, bought oranges from the natives, and settled down in third-class carriages of a filthy and uncomfortable kind. Each horse truck bore a chalked date of when it had last been disinfected, but the carriages had no such reassuring legend. As darkness fell, the train started with a series of crashes, and clanked unpromisingly away into the gloom. It was a weary journey, and bitterly cold. Mac could not sleep and watched, by the silver light of the waning moon, a not displeasing *vista* of palm trees, crops, houses and villages which went jogging steadily by.

Twice they crossed great rivers, and the whole carriage bestirred itself to see its first of what might be the Nile. Then there were many railway junctions and tall houses and a tram-car or two, and again country. At midnight the train jolted finally to a halt. They led their horses out into a sandy square surrounded by houses and palm-trees. Mac noticed that they were wandering unaware over what apparently were Nile mud bricks set out to dry in the sun. Some poor native, he thought, would curse the war next day.

The column of tired horses and tired men wandered vaguely off to find the camp, barracks or what-not which should prove to be their destination. No one knew who it was, where it was or what it was, and there was no guide. They took a turning to the right, passed a convent, took other turnings and found nothing but shuttered houses among trees peacefully asleep in the moonlight. There was no living thing, and the hollow echo of their own clatter was the only sound. They were all more or less asleep, and just wandered along, not caring a hang whether they walked or halted, or stood on their heads.

In due course they passed the same old convent, which, in Mac's sleepy mind, did not seem to be quite the right thing to be doing, though he did not mind much. Eventually the column encountered a high iron railing barring its path—a great iron railing stretching for miles and inside it a camp. They found troughs and watered the horses, and picketed them along the railings. There was someone in the camp, and the squadron was told to stay by its horses till morning.

It was colder than Mac had ever felt it. A great stillness held everything, and the moon lit the sleeping camp with a clear soft light. But it was cold! After the warm tropic weeks, the keen Egyptian winter night went right to the marrow. Mac tried to bury himself in the sand by scooping a long hole, lying in it and shovelling the sand back over him. It was not a success, and there was nothing to do but pace up and down in a vain endeavour to get warm.

Hours passed in a dreamy fashion until at length Mac's attention was drawn by signs of activity in the camp. He went there and found some cooks round their dixies and iron rails in the open just starting a fire. He immediately made friends, and speedily assisted the fire to become a respectable blaze. Others came from the squadron and soon the cooks were hospitably handing out mugs of tea and bread for toast. It was the camp of the Lancashire Artillery, Mac learned, who had arrived from England a month since. The sergeant-cook soon joined the great-coated circle round the fire.

"Yus," he said, with the confidence of a host to whom deference should be paid, "Yus. Hi 'eard as 'ow them Noo Zealanders wus comin', an' I says ter meself as 'ow it 'ud be another o' these 'ere lingos we'd 'av ter try an' parley. An' I think's as 'ow that don't suit us chaps zactly. But the fust of you fellers I sees this mornin' I says ter 'im like, 'Goo' mornin,' maate!' An' 'e says ter me 'Goo' mornin,' maate,' jest the same as meself! We thought as 'ow you'd talk some funny lingo, I tell yer I did. But yuse jest speak same's us, an' I wus glad."

Daylight revealed a scene as inspiring to an untravelled New Zealander as America to Columbus. Close at hand stood an oriental city of splendid architecture, the early light touching with romance its minarets and pillared galleries. Spread before him, and stretching away into the distance until lost in a soft blue mistiness, lay Cairo, its forest of minarets, its domes and its square-topped houses. Beyond, unmistakable in the blue distance, were the old familiar outlines of the great pyramids. Behind him, the great yellow desert spread away to the horizon and the rising sun, and was bordered on the other hand by a forest of palm trees, almost hiding many fine houses with shady courts and playing fountains.

The sun soon brought warmth into the troopers' frozen limbs, and they went to work watering and feeding the horses. Later in the morning they moved to the site of the camp to be, about a mile away. It was a wind-smoothed stretch of untouched desert, but speedily horse-lines and white tents broke its vastness. That night Mac, doing his turn of horse-picket while the tired camp slept, walked out a little way into the silver moonlit desert. In the utter stillness, with the cold pure air, the sands unmarked by any footstep, and the impression of unlimited space, the desert seemed a new world—a world far away from the old one.

But busy days followed, and the desert soon lost its first charm in the solid practical work of leading the horses across it on foot till they should be strong enough to be ridden again. It was hot dusty work in the midday sun, and Mac was thankful when the day came for him to hoist his lazy bones into the saddle. The camp grew, and became a place of importance with its great piles of stores, its roads and its rows of mean speedily-erected shops of Greek, Armenian and Egyptian cheap-jacks. The troops quickly fell in with the life, and set out to make the most of Egypt and its pleasures.

They were there until the end of April, and in those five months Mac saw most of the country one way or another, though all his journeyings are not chronicled in the pages to come. In the course of time he hated the place, and longed with the rest of the mounted men to pass to new fields and fresh adventures. But he looks back now on those Egyptian days as the jolliest days there ever were, and breathes a sigh of sorrow that they can never come again.

CHAPTER 6
Days in the Desert

Mac felt absolutely dejected, and looked it. His mare, too, appeared neither happy nor spirited. Except for some nebulous figures, indistinct in the yellow murk, little else was visible. Mac crouched scowling in the lee of the mare, who stood with drooping head and closed eyes, swaying occasionally to the violent buffetings of the desert storm, and patiently waiting for some move on the part of her master. The three squadrons and the transport had left camp independently just after dawn with instructions to bivouac together, at midday, at a certain spot known to the High Command by the enigmatical formula "No. 3. Tower, 105°—Virgin's Breasts 45°."

Mac, who carried the compass, had taken various bearings before the breaking of the storm, and had now halted where the major and he considered angles, bearings, and letters indicated. There was no sign of the other units. Either they had sagaciously abandoned the expedition earlier or else they had other opinions regarding the trysting place. Anyhow, whether they were still wandering about the infernal desert or not, Mac was firmly convinced that camp was the place for him. Picking up his rein, he made in the direction of a blur he knew to be the major, and told him so. The major had visions of pleasant refuge in a Cairene hotel, a good dinner, and a cool bath, instead of a night trek in the desert as originally intended. So, he agreed, and shrill whistling stirred to life more or less comatose troopers and horses.

Steering, nor'-nor'-west, each following close upon the next ahead, they rode in deep silence. They crossed wave after wave of sand-hills, monotonous and bewildering. The *khamsin* blew in hot, sandy spurts, and lulled; then came again in hotter, more shrivelling bursts "From Hell!" thought the troopers, one and all. Sand trickled down their necks, and filtered down to that place where it neither increased the comfort of their riding nor diminished the ardour of their revilings against the weather. With fiercer gusts, gravel rose and stung horse and rider, while the former stumbled frequently over unseen boulders.

In the latter half of the afternoon they struck the old railway embankment to Suez, lost it again, but soon found the edge of the irrigated land and followed it to the camp. Parched, red-eyed, headachy, and yellow with dust, they made for their lines, watered their horses, and set about making themselves as comfortable as circumstances allowed. The happiness of the trooper was not enhanced when he failed to find a misty blur representing his tent. It had chosen to give up the unequal contest and had departed down-wind. He followed, and joined the rest of the tent's company in recovering the tattered remnants, and towels, and personal property which had strayed into the domain of the next regiment.

Camp was not a healthy spot in the *khamsin* days, Mac decided. Coins to a *piastreless* cobber smoothed over a horse-picket difficulty, and he passed out of the camp by back ways. So, in the village of Helmeih, he spent the night. Gusts bellowed through the swaying date-palms overhead, and roared round the courtyard, but his bed was comfortable, and the house of his good French friends proof against the sand-laden blasts of the spring storm. He was awakened sufficiently early to allow of his appearance at roll-call next morning. It was not according to his nature to rise early from so pleasant a bed, but it was a matter of discretion.

Many days were passed in the desert, none worse and many better. Troop days were all right; squadron days were not bad; regimental days were tolerable at times; but brigade and divisional manoeuvres were inventions of the devil. On these latter occasions, elusive white flags, the skeleton enemy, appeared and disappeared. Scouts reported them here, then there. The mounted men advanced in open order, all except the front line smothered in a fog of dust.

Infantry toiled and sweated after them. The maligned staff viewed from afar the battle royal. Thankful men received wounds from galloping umpires, and lay down peacefully to await rescue by the attentive ambulance. Chastisements descended from great to lesser dignitaries. Why had not Colonel Macpherson managed to move his flank-guard three miles in two minutes?

So, a field day would pass, each rank being roundly condemned to everlasting perdition by the rank immediately below it, until the G.O.C., Egypt, and the British Empire, bore the brunt of the awful damnings. Bad-tempered and dishevelled, the troops would set off on their homeward march, the final straw being added to the annoyances of the infantry by the passage to windward of the mounted rifles. Shrouded in the dust, they levelled their final, terrible threats against those who would be home two hours before them.

Times there were, too, good times, when the troopers would trek across the Delta to the Barrage du Nil, a pleasant spot where the Nile divides into its delta streams and canals. Here they would bivouac for the night beneath shady plantations of *lebbak* trees in beautiful gardens. In the daytime they swam their horses in the river. A jolly form of amusement there was the blanket-tossing of intruding natives, who were rather prone to contract those things which did not belong to them; and no method of discouragement was so efficacious. The "*Gyppies*" were fleet of foot, but so were the troopers, and to see a lanky southerner pursuing a victim was good entertainment. Captured at length and shrieking in abject terror, they would go flying skyward from the tautened blanket. But, alas, the blankets were of government manufacture, and occasionally, upon the victim's meteoric return, would split in two. Thus, many blankets were rent in twain, and thus did many dusky ones learn that the belongings of the troopers were sacred property.

And so Egyptian days passed light-heartedly enough. That was before the serious times, before they had been involved in the real fierce thing. And now few of them ride together any longer. Many will ride no more, and others are scattered over the earth.

CHAPTER 7

Mac Goes to Cairo

The camp lay listless in the glaring heat of high noon. Long rows of tents gleamed dazzlingly in the sun. Saddlery, horse-rugs, nose-bags and gear were untidily scattered about. Except for the sleepy figure of the horse-picket, attempting vainly to keep his lanky person within the shadow of the feed-trough, there was no one in sight. The horses needed little attention. With heads low and legs crooked, they dozed in every attitude of *siesta*. Within the open tents lay the human element, more or less replete after the seldom varying meal of sandy stew and bread. Most of the men slept, stretched full length upon rush matting on the shady sides of the tents. Some wore trousers, some shirts and some neither.

Stretched full length upon his back, his head supported upon his neighbour's chest, and his eyes idly following the ceaseless procession of flies round the tent pole, Mac smoked and pondered deeply: was it worth the fag to go to Cairo? Knowing full well that his last three weeks' shirts and socks awaited washing, he decidedly dutifully to remain at home, though possibly he might take the air, and probably the beer, of Heliopolis in the evening. However, his good intentions were ruthlessly upset, for at that moment the interior of his desert domicile was swiftly converted into a swirling tornado of dust and dirt. Blankets, towels and hay departed upwards, and all was turmoil. In five seconds, the air was calm again, but not so the eight inhabitants of the canvas home.

Emerging from repose and a fog of grimy dust, they condemned Egypt and things Egyptian in no uncertain tones. They had washed and eaten, and had settled down comfortably for the afternoon, and why had this confounded blanky cyclone selected their blanky tent to blanky well empty itself upon! Often during the midday heat, "weary Willies," swirling spiral columns of sand 1,000 feet high, wandered in slow procession along the edge of the desert from the north-east, usually missing the camp, but sometimes crossing it, leaving a narrow trail of chaos and ill temper. Mac met the situation with admirable dignity and philosophy. This disturbance decided the Cairo question—he would go. Still muttering wrathfully, the tent's complement sought their individual towels and gravitated independently and sorrowfully towards the shower-baths.

Three-quarters of an hour later found Mac, suitably adorned, sitting on a bench at Helmeih Station having his boots and *bandolier* polished by four jabbering, disreputable "*Gyppie*" youngsters, who swore glibly the while the most lurid English oaths. Incidentally, they often terminated an exceptionally fluent flow with "Eh, Mistah Mickkenzie?" the usual mode of native address to New Zealanders after the High Commissioner's visit, which sometimes ruffled Mac's dignity, but more often amused him. His toilet was cut short by the arrival of the train, so, seizing *bandolier* and spurs and dropping a few coins, he jumped into a second-class compartment with but one boot clean of desert sand.

Rattling through Palais de Koubbeh and Demerdache, he considered what he might do with himself now he had quitted camp. Money was not so plentiful as in those palmy days when they had set foot in this Orient land with two months' pay behind them. "Special prices," too, were quoted for these men from the south. However, it was a lot of trouble to think on such an afternoon; he would decide it later. At any rate a shave was felt to be the most overpowering necessity, though, really, the desert did make one thirsty! A shave would be the second item.

In a small inferior *café* near the Boulak Station, he discovered Jock, an artilleryman he knew, and together they satisfied their thirst; neither had formed any plan for the afternoon, so both welcomed the idea of spending it in company. They adjourned to the barber's. Shaving in Sahara sand appealed not to Mac's heart, and, failing visits to Cairo, mornings found him in an evil mood with a painful task before him.

Shaving over, and Mac's other boot cleaned, a little sight-seeing was suggested as a modest and inexpensive way of passing the afternoon. The pyramids were stale, besides being a dickens of a distance off. The gunner voted for the citadel, and Mac didn't mind, though he had been there once already. They made their way towards a gharry stand, and, spurning clamouring drivers from their path, comfortably seated themselves in the one which appeared to sport the best pair of Arab horses. Their feet supported upon the opposite seat, blue wisps of the best Egyptian tobacco smoke trailing over the hood behind, they set off. Scanning the Oriental life surging round them, criticizing

Arab methods of dressing sheep, amused by the scribes and money-changers—dirty though prosperous-looking sharpers—and so on and so forth, they passed slowly down the long Sharia-Mahommed Ali, between the frowning walls of two great Mosques, where the cannon balls of Napoleon are still fast in the stone, and then up the sharp incline into the citadel itself.

Leaving the Arab driver in a paroxysm of tears because he had received only one-third more than his lawful fare, Jock and Mac passed by the sentries, through the cavernous mouth of the main gate into the inner precincts of the Citadel. How powerful a fortress in days gone by it must have been, they thought, but how short lived and unavailing it would prove before modern artillery. They came to a halt before the great Mosque of Mahommed Ali, and the fine, tapering minarets met with their deepest approval.

At the entrance they assumed the apologetic sandals and were taken in hand by an obtrusive dragoman, who, besides impressing them with his own importance, related with small appreciation of truth fabulous facts concerning the edifice. They duly noted his salient pronouncements, rewarded him with a few *piastres* and "*imshi yallah'ed*" in duet when he demanded more. Then, in the late afternoon sunlight, they stood on the edge of the cliff without. There they talked of many things while looking out over that weird, mysterious city, over its forests of graceful minarets, towards the green delta beyond; across the Nile to the west where the Pyramids of Gizeh stood silhouetted against the setting sun, and down into the gloom in the valley to the east, where, silent and deserted, lay the City of the Dead.

Stirred into activity once more by feelings of emptiness and thoughts of their weekly square meal, they turned their backs upon the glory of the Egyptian evening and wandered down to the depths again. They jostled their way through the throng, human and animal, which made progress difficult and the atmosphere strong. Spotting a couple of donkeys in the charge of one Arab donkey boy, they schemed with each other with a view to his undoing.

"Very gude, Noo Zealand," said the dusky one when approached. "Gib it twenty *piastres* for stashion."

"All right, ole sport. You'll get it at t'other end, and make your blanky bone-bags go. Savvy?"

They proceeded fairly satisfactorily at first, Ahmed only having to be occasionally reprimanded for not producing sufficient speed on the part of his donks. Then, while the Arab was in front of Mac, vainly endeavouring to persuade Jock's mount to proceed less swiftly, Mac quietly took a turning to the left. The Arab went twenty-five yards farther before he missed him. In violent excitement he tore after him and besought him to stop.

"All right, you black diamond," said Mac cheerfully, and remained standing in the street.

The Arab, his fears at rest, chased the other soldier, but as soon as the native had disappeared round the corner, Mac moved on again. The same thing happened in the case of the gunner, who halted immediately the Arab arrived. The latter wanted to lead the donkey in the direction of the trooper, but the gunner was obstinate and insisted that his was the correct way. In a frame of mind too horrible to contemplate, the Arab disappeared once more in pursuit of the trooper, only to find he had entirely evaporated. In the throes of the greatest dilemma of his life he returned, to learn that the worst had come to pass and the gunner and his donkey also were gone from his sight.

"*Allah!* Oh, *Allah!*" he wailed, and, burying his head in his long blue skirts, he dissolved into tears.

By devious ways Mac and Jock journeyed onwards, until, happy and laughing at having for once done a nigger in the eye, they rejoined at the Obelisk Restaurant, where they turned their borrowed steeds adrift. Coming weekly as it did, dinner in Cairo was an affair of some length, and, between shandies and cigarettes, it was already late when it was *mafeesh.* They strolled along the streets and were about to drop into the Café Egyptien, when they espied a fellow-countryman struggling with a donkey. They went to his assistance, to discover that the donk-man was, quite unnecessarily, attempting to stop a bottle of beer being poured down the donk's throat.

This promised sport, so Jock quickly procured four more bottles of cheap beer and they joined the third soldier in his estimable effort. Abdul had secured an assistant against this vile outrage to his animal, but he was temporarily put out of action by having the reins made fast round his lower extremities.

The donk rapidly absorbed three bottles, while the distracted "*Gyppies*" tugged and wailed, "No gude! No gude! Finish Noo Zealand!" to which the only reply was "*Imshi Yallah,* you black devils." At this stage the little beast, an animal of rather miserable dimensions, with a large, rotund centrepiece, escaped and wobbled ridiculously down the street. He was recaptured, drenched with two more bottles, and let loose to wander wherever his tottery legs would carry him.

The donk swayed and stumbled, his ears cocked at all angles, and his expression happy and foolish. The gathered soldiers laughed till their sides were sore, and when tired of this fun they let the Arabs take away, as best they could, their ill-used, though happy, ass.

The hour had grown late. To the station the trooper and the gunner wended their way. A short sleep in the train, a tired walk campwards in the clear coolness of the Egyptian night, and to bed on the open sand beneath a starry vault. "Lights out" sounded clearly in their camp, and echoed more beautifully and faintly from other camps along the desert's edge.

CHAPTER 8

Mac Tours in Comfort

Mac sighed appreciatively. If Egypt was to be seen, this was undoubtedly the way to see it. On the whole it had been an exceedingly profitable little bit of diplomacy, coupled with good luck, that had attached him to a party of distinguished people, whose privilege it was to be shown Egypt as the government chose to show it. He lay comfortably in his bed smoking. Travelling in this manner appealed to him. His first tastes of Egyptian railway travelling, in dirty, clanking boxes, which required disinfecting, had not been pleasant. Now, from the darkened cabin of a saloon car on the *Cairo-Luxor express de luxe*, he watched the fleeting *vista* of moonlit palms, sleeping villages, and silhouetted hills.

He had left New Zealand some six months before with the intention of slaying Germans, not of touring in luxury in Egypt, but he was not averse to these interim enjoyments. The war could wait, and anyhow at that particular moment it was hardly showing any inclination of stopping, and neither was Zeitoun Camp a place of unmixed blessings. Arrived at this state of mental satisfaction, he threw the remnants of his cigarette out of the window and went to sleep.

When he awoke, they were rattling over a Nile bridge, and the sun shone full in upon him. The early morning scene of industrious blue-robed fellaheen at work in the green fields, the graceful palms, desert hills, and blue sky thrilled the one artistic fibre which had strayed into his soul. He shaved at leisure, bathed luxuriously, dressed, and met the other four members of the party in the saloon for breakfast. Towards the end of the meal they steamed into Luxor, where once stood the ancient and wonderful Theban capital.

Here many days were passed, investigating tombs and temples of all shapes and sizes; great and wonderful hieroglyphics were explained, though these left the trooper cold. They rode on donkeys deep into the deserts, followed by Sudanese guards on fine Arab steeds.

From Luxor they duly departed in the direction of Assuan. The direct distance was not over-long, but the day was blazing hot, the railway was badly constructed, and the sand filtered steadily into the cars. It was a comic-opera railway, this narrow-gauge line. The contract for its construction was let at an exceedingly profitable rate per mile to a French company. More miles meant more money, so naturally they spun the thing out and consequently for no apparent reason, the line zigzags across perfectly level stretches of desert.

Assuan at last. Great *nabobs* bowed; Mac saluted. The honoured guests would take the State gharries to their hotel? No? Walk! Impossible! Great people did not walk. It took much gentle persuasion to convey to the *mahmoudieh*—the governor of the province—that the guests wished to take exercise, now that the cool of the evening was come. His Excellency was a gentleman of portly proportions, who, at some other period, may have walked. Despite his dimensions, he was agile and graceful in his sweeping *salaams*; when he spoke, he emphasized every word with an appropriate sweep of the arm, and his eyebrows arched and his eyes bulged in superlative, ecstatic moments.

The tassel of his *tarboosh*, a little red inverted flowerpot capping the summit, gyrated violently in moments of excitement. Altogether he was a mighty person. Perceiving this, the five great ones from the far south paid court to him, addressed him "Your Excellency this" and "Your Excellency that"; and paid tribute to his lands, to his people, and his province, and expressed a desire to see his wives. The *mahmoudieh* visibly swelled with pleasure.

Assuan was duly investigated. Much like Luxor, it consisted of a terrace along the riverbank, of hotels, some clean and comfortable, some Greek; foreign consulates and banks. Gardens, shaded by palms and *lebbak*-trees, made this portion of the town quite habitable. Behind, on the rising sand-dunes, lay the crowded, stifling mass of native dwellings, to visit which one's heart must be strong. Bazaars might be artistic and unique, but as their quaintness and picturesqueness increased so also did the odours of garlic, the uncleanliness, and the flies in their myriads.

Time passed pleasantly in Assuan, though at length Mac thought they had about exhausted most of its possibilities. There were mosques, temples and bazaars; there was a wild race of desert Bisharin, whose living was precarious in those days of war, since they had existed by dancing weird, wild dances for the enlightenment of tourists; there was a museum, rather a mouldy place like their kind, where were relics of ages untold, and, much to Mac's amusement, a mummified sheep. He thought the New Zealand method of freezing much more practicable.

At length, one morning, ere the mist wraiths had vanished, they crawled slowly southwards across the rich golden sand of the lower Sudanese desert. It was pleasantly bracing and clear in the early desert morning, and Mac felt light-hearted and happy, as he gazed across the distant featureless dunes of sand. Successfully accomplishing a non-stop run of twenty miles in an hour and a half, they arrived at Shellal, a village of a few mud huts and a station, a jetty with a steamer or two, which took travellers farther to the south, to Wadi Haifa and Khartoum.

About the place itself there was little of interest; it was a one-horse show with a few Arabs, Bedouins and Sudanese, many flea-bitten mongrels and clouds of flies. But this island-studded expanse of water was the great Assuan Dam. The gates had been closed at this season for about a month, and the rising tide had just reached the floor of the beautiful Temple of Isis, which stood, half a mile away, perfectly reflected in the calm waters.

They wheezed away over to it in a steam pinnace, got temporarily snagged on the top of a stray pillar, and eventually disembarked from their hissing, modern contraption at the very portals, where oft times Cleopatra and her suite were wont to enter from their state barges. Mac's rather hazy notions of that lady wrapped her in a halo of romance, and now he walked the lovely aisles which she had trod. Was it, he thought, worthwhile gradually to spoil this wonderful building for the sake of *lucre* from twentieth century Egypt?

From the old they went to the new, landing at the eastern end of the great granite wall that bars the Nile at the head of the foaming first cataract. Natives pushed them in trollies along the top of the mile wall. Water roared in great white jets through the sluices, tempering the blistering heat of the midday hours. It was a wonderful work, this dam, a great peaceful desert lake above and a turbulent flood below. They descended by a flight of locks to the quieter water, and steamed ten or fifteen miles downstream between many islands of red granite, smoothly polished by the rushing waters of countless centuries. Back again at Assuan, they embarked on a luxurious river steamer, the

Sakkara, and immediately cast off, for down river.

This method of seeing the country took a lot of beating, meditated Mac, as he lounged back in a low chair on the cool deck, with his sleeves rolled up, smoking a cigar. The life of the Nile riverbank was deeply interesting, with a slightly varying background of green fields of *berseem*, stately palms and rocky desert hills. How cool the palms looked, but he knew from experience that the degree of shade ascribed to them in romantic novels didn't exist in real life. Lulled by the steady reverberations of the paddle-wheels, conscious internally of a satisfying lunch and good wine, he fell asleep. When he awoke, they were manoeuvring carefully up to the bank, and black sailors in Jack Tar uniform quickly extemporised a landing out of planks.

Drawn up on top of the bank, brightly polished and perspiring, stood a line of dusky soldiers, presenting arms. At the end of the gang-plank, his portliness exceeded only by his stateliness, was the great potentate His Excellency the Mahmoudieh of Assuan. With sweeping obeisances, he greeted each one in a manner only befitting those who held his provinces in such deep respect. His demeanour demanded rather a setting of pillared palace and crimson velvet than a background of castor-oil bushes and sugar-cane.

But he did things properly, did the *mahmoudieh*, showed them Kom Ombo Temple, with all the dignity of the proprietor, took them to his sugar-mills in his best donkey-drawn tram-car, and offered them almost everything in his dominions. Finally, when they re-embarked farther downstream, they warmly bade farewell to the old boy, told him emphatically of the unapproachability of his province, and bowed and waved handkerchiefs until beyond a bend in the river they lost sight of his memorable shape.

That night the steamer lay moored to the bank near the native town of Edfu. The skipper was considerably concerned, as he explained with violent gesticulations, at the possibility of being stranded on the morrow, as the season of low Nile was at hand. To Mac a day or two in the middle of the river was a matter of little moment. The quarters were comfortable, and Zeitoun Camp was no place towards which to hurry. So, unmoved by the skipper's anxieties, he retired to the lower deck, and praised the engines to the Sudanese engineer until that gentleman beamed with pride and his teeth glistened white in the dusk.

In the early hours soon after dawn, they went on donkeys to the Temple of Edfu. The morning was mysterious and foreboding. Over the whole country a weird silence reigned and wrapped the towering walls of the ancient temple in eeriness; there were no clouds, but the sun was like a great red moon, and all the landscape enveloped in an orange gloom. They rode in silence, awed strangely by Nature's will. Animals were restive and gloomy too. They returned to breakfast aboard when the steamer cast off, and proceeded down river. Soon a hot breath of wind came from the south, on which great columns of sand swept over the desert. The gale increased, puffs blew as from a fiery furnace; the sun became obscured altogether, and soon also the river banks.

Bored by the gloom of his fellow-voyagers and depressed, Mac betook himself to his state-room, and went to sleep. He woke for lunch, went once more to sleep, awoke again in the evening when Luxor was reached, and hastened through the squalid streets to board the saloon car for Cairo. Even in the gale and the fog of sand the skipper had not managed to find a convenient mud-bank on which to ground his steamer, and Mac told him he didn't think he was much of a sport.

He had enjoyed Upper Egypt, especially journeying in so comfortable a manner, but, after all, it wouldn't be bad fun seeing the boys again, even if they were at Zeitoun Camp.

CHAPTER 9
Mac Lunches with the Sultan

In the glaring heat of the Egyptian high-noon hours a car drew up outside the large hotel in the Sharia Kamel and a more or less soiled and weather-beaten trooper alighted. He made his way up the steps, across the shady terrace and into the dim cool depths of the pillared hall. He had been to an excessively sandy inspection that morning somewhere in the Sahara, and now his mien betokened appreciative anticipation of a refresher to his dusty throat. After that a wash would go rather well, perhaps a cigarette, and then lunch. But, alas, no such luck! Apparently, something out of the ordinary was afoot. Even the dignity of the heavy-weight, superior, self-satisfied, alleged Swiss *maitre d'hotel* was for the moment disturbed. Native *s'fragis*, neglecting their work, were voluble, gesticulatory, but quite unintelligible.

Finally, Mac was led to understand that His Serene Highness the *Sultan*, learning of his presence at the hotel, had made known the Imperial wish that he desired to honour the trooper by entertaining him to lunch. However, there had been grave difficulties in putting the whole affair in order. Mac had left early for the desert inspection, and several envoys, calling in regular succession, had been unable to learn his Christian name. Moreover, it had been deemed necessary to obtain the assurance of the general officer commanding in Egypt that it would be quite in order to invite a trooper to the palace of His Serene Highness. But those small difficulties were duly overcome, and now, twenty minutes before the appointed hour, an extremely gorgeous and majestic person presented Mac with the serene invitation.

Now, he had considered it an extravagance to arise sufficiently early to permit of his being shaved before the parade. Also, his garments, which had wallowed in the mud of Takapau Camp many months ago, were constructed for a person of smaller dimensions, and his generous government had not taken into consideration such occasions as *Sultans'* luncheon parties, when designing the uniform. These were small matters in his mind, and if the *Sultan's* Imperial wish was to be granted, he should have the trooper, beard, uniform and all. So, with the immediate dust of the desert removed and with a borrowed but ancient shako upon his head, he was *salaamed* down the steps again with unusual pomp and flourish.

The royal equipage conveyed him with much dignity down the long Sharia Abdin and across the great open square to the palace entrance. As he entered, he acknowledged the salute of the gaudy guard in just that off-hand manner befitting a bush-country shepherd. He was much bowed into a great room where there was an epidemic of liveried darkies, a grand chamberlain or so and a few Cabinet Ministers.

In common with the rest, he was subjected to a thorough spring-cleaning with feather dusters. Before imperturbable and mighty chamberlains, up to his ankles in crimson carpet and generally struck with the magnificence of his surroundings, Mac for a moment lost his nerve, but speedily recovering himself, informed a *tarbooshed* individual that it was a fine day. Unfortunately, this conversation did not prove fruitful, for, besides the fact that the subject of the weather in Egypt is a quickly exhausted topic, the gentleman to whom the remark had been addressed soon made it evident that he failed to comprehend. However, the trooper soon unearthed a magnificently emblazoned official from the Sudan, who happened to be English, and struck up an acquaintance with him.

A nervous plucking of garments on the part of some of the company indicated that the prelude was near an end. Slowly the assembly was ushered from the room, along a hall, up a wonderful staircase, and at last into the august presence of His Serene Highness. Mac took note of the contortions through which his predecessors passed, made his bow and shook hands with becoming dignity, muttered once more that the day was fine, and backed across the room. All stood round the chamber, and talked about nothing to no one. Others entered and did their gymnastics, until the room contained the whole Cabinet, all portly persons in *tarbooshes*, the afore-mentioned Sudan gentleman, and a few British people, one in khaki. Now came the real thing.

All in order, according to their great greatness or their lesser greatness, filed from the room, Mac bringing up the rear. The dining-room was an apartment of a gorgeousness, the like of which he had not seen before. He was accorded the gentleman from the Sudan on one side, and a cabinet minister with an unpronounceable name on the other. The table was oval and loaded with a munificence of delicacies on dishes of gold and silver and a riot of strange exotic flowers.

The epidemic of servants in post-impressionist attire had spread to the dining-hall. Savoury dishes of rare and exceeding excellence appeared and disappeared in rapid procession. Dusky men switched one dish silently away before Mac had half tasted its delights and promptly replaced it by another. Breakfast was some distance in the rear and this food of kings was more to his palate than sand stew "*à la Zeitun,*" and the wine stood high in comparison to the watered beer of Ind, Coope. So, all went well. The gentleman from the Sudan talked of many things, and Mac told him nearly all about God's own country. The cabinet minister chipped in occasionally, but scarcely seemed to comprehend the vastness of a sheep station with 200,000 sheep and only a score of shepherds to tend them.

Coffee came, cigars followed, and the trooper made hay while the sun shone.

Eventually a retreat was made to the ante-room. The haze of tobacco smoke filled the place, and those who had a language in common spoke cordially one to the other. At length a thrill ran instinctively, it seemed, through the company, and all became severely courtly once more. Chamberlains took up their accustomed places, people said formal things to each other; obeisances were indulged in, hands shaken, courteous remarks made, and thus the company gradually evaporated. Mac's turn came.

Before His Serene Highness he successfully accomplished his sweeping earthward curves, thanked the *Sultan* for his kindness, but, unaccustomed to the retrograde manner of leaving a room backwards, he unfortunately found that the door was in the wrong place, and met the wall with a resounding thwack. However, it was all in the game, even though he did not think much of this method of quitting a room. So, leaving by the normal mode, he was soon back in the old spring-cleaning room, being *salaamed*, his hat and appurtenances being returned to him with the usual Oriental ceremony.

Mac was not quite certain of the rest of the programme and was somewhat surprised to find that the next act was the meeting at the station of the New High Commissioner for Egypt. However, why not? It was all very interesting and there was one of the Sultan's cars waiting. So, waving a return salute to the Sudanese guard, as it presented arms, he embarked upon this next little jaunt.

Away through the sun-baked Abdin Square again, back along the Sharia and past the Ezbekieh, he was soon passing down the narrow lane between throngs of garlic-scented humanity. At the great iron gates of the Boulak Station, the car with the trooper, solitary and dignified within, entered the avenue of Sphinx-like dragoons, well-polished and groomed. This led to a square lined with infantry. In the centre on one side was the royal door thrown wide, towards which stretched a broad ribbon of crimson carpet. The car came to a standstill. Nothing daunted, the trooper descended in solitary state. An unearthly silence held the throng and to Mac the carpet seemed interminable, but at last it ended, and, passing through the cavernous, gloomy opening, he was soon swallowed up in a great crowd of mighty dignitaries. Acres of the same crimson carpet covered the platform, its far limits bordered by khaki soldiers.

On it moved a kaleidoscopic gallery of *tarbooshes*, red tabs and top hats. Never before had top hats been used officially in Egypt, and, resurrected from long neglect, were mostly relics of a past decade. Mac thought they were about as suitable for the climate as a cellular shirt in the Antarctic. Most of the company looked rather bored, and he could find no one to speak to, for all were apparently inwardly dwelling too much upon costume and coming formalities.

The train was late. They grew still more bored. At last, hideously decorated with flags and shrubbery, it rattled in, hissing and steaming. From a saloon carriage stepped the new arrival, garbed in court apparel. Taken in charge by some great officials, he was being introduced to all and sundry. Mac rather wondered under what high title, he, a mere private, might be introduced.

Among all the mighty men there, the only one he knew was his army corps commander; so, placing himself at that gentleman's back, he awaited events. Slowly the lengthy procedure went on, and slowly the bobbing and bowing grew closer. At length, clad in clothes of finest silk, the great man came before the general and his staff, when in due course with a graceful sweep of his feathered hat he acknowledged the introduction of Mac as one of the general staff. In the course of time it was all over.

Out through the great porch again, out into the air the great people passed and dispersed. Mac neglected His Serene Highness's Imperial conveyance and sought a common taxi, went down the khaki lanes and back to his hotel. There once more he gained a secluded corner, ordered a drink and unbuttoned the collar of his tunic.

The *Sultan* did not forget his guest, Mac. Amidst all his busy life, he heard, nine months later, that his trooper lay wounded and sick in a hospital at Alexandria. He despatched an envoy to express his deepest sympathy, his hopes for better health, and a desire to know the extent of his wounds. Then, when Mac reached England, the *Sultan* sent further messages and inquiries concerning the trooper whom he had honoured at his table at the Abdin Palace.

CHAPTER 10

Mac Disapproves of Being Left

Mac felt fed up. The worst had come to pass. The infantry had gone away and left them, the mounted men, to sweat and swear in the desert till the war was over, and Heaven only knew when that would be. He had been on fatigue today for not getting up until an hour after reveille, and he was in no temper to be trifled with. A foolish non-com. had taken the fatigue party to the wrong depot, where the O.C., opposed on principle to a fine body of men wanting for work, saw that they were not wasted.

After a morning's work, just as they were about to retire for lunch, the peppery officer who had been foaming all the morning about his missing men appeared and claimed them, and refused to dismiss them before they had done his job as well. In the almost unbearable heat, the party, rebellious and wrathful, had straggled off to the railway station, where a heavy afternoon's work loomed before them. Saturday afternoon too, and no dinner! Work! They didn't think! So, they retreated to a shady *café*, and, despite the expostulations of the corporal, lunched upon the one satiating thing the place contained—beer.

This did not fit them for an afternoon on a tropical day, so that, when the zealous officer came at five to view the completed work, he found only a collection of happy and sleepy warriors pleasantly reclining in the shade of a *tibbin* stack. Awful threats fell unheeded upon them, and the work remained undone. Further refreshed, they meandered homewards, attempted vainly to maintain a comparatively straight line while they were dismissed by an amused sergeant-major, and retired to their lines to prepare for a Cairene evening.

Mac firmly resolved things had come to a pass when something dire had to be done. He adjourned to the lines of another regiment, and consulted, nay, intrigued, with his cobber. The result was that each one's officer was approached by a trooper, who made clear the vital necessity of his visiting the site of ancient Memphis and the Tombs of Sakkara on the morrow. This was in the interests of his archaeological researches, and he pleaded special leave. One officer only came up to scratch, which was but a minor difficulty. Other means could be resorted to for ensuring comparative safety. Military police and some of the sergeants, especially if friends, were not averse to persuasion.

So, it came to pass that eight o'clock the following morning found them dodging military policemen and staff officers on a platform of the Boulak station. They succeeded in ensconcing themselves in the Alexandria express without much difficulty, the only incidents being the upsetting of the equilibrium of a native railway official, a guard or so, and a few porters. Alexandria at eleven. Their first act was to satisfy their long-standing appetites. Then to the docks they went, to fulfil, if possible, their mission, which was not archaeological research, but to follow their infantry to the north. They searched along the quays to see if any possibility offered of slipping aboard an outbound transport. Alas, the only vessel there cast off while they, barred by a hopeless line of sentries, gazed sadly on. They hired a Greek sailing-boat, to investigate the vessels in harbour, but were only marooned by him on an American warship. They would know better next time than to trust a Greek and pay him first.

Relieved later in the afternoon from this predicament, the troopers betook themselves once more to the French *café*, where, enamoured of the *mam'selle*, time passed pleasantly. "*Café*, chocolate, and *demoiselles très bonne oui*." At any rate, if they had missed escaping from Egypt, there were worse ways than this of spending the day.

Late at night, tired, *piastreless*, and with forebodings of the mat, but happy and careless, they arrived back in Cairo. By devious ways they reached their camp and their tents; and spread their blankets in the open, under the stars. There was probably a large dose of fatigue in store, and a few hours would see the rise of the sun over the sand-hills to the east, the dawn of another day of heat, dust, flies, and work. But they had given play to their spirits; and so, with the philosophy of the average bush-whacker and stockman, they went contentedly to sleep.

CHAPTER 11

Mac Leaves for Active Service

Egypt blistered in the early summer heat; flies increased in myriads; clouds of locusts darkened the sky; and hot winds blew, scorching and parching everything. The infantry had vanished to the north, to perilous adventures in the unknown; and the mounted men were grieved to the very depths of their souls to be left thus behind to stagnate on this sun-baked Sahara. The days passed monotonously, with perpetual grooming and exercising, and the noonday hours spent beneath the palms, alleged to be shady.

Cairo was a past delight. Its romance had gone; the weird mystery of the Oriental city had lost its fascination; and no incense-laden, music-haunted, brightly-coloured corner remained unexplored. Cairo was wonderful; but Cairo was filthy. The troopers had tasted of its delights, and were satiated.

Grousing was rife in the camp and the troopers were nervy. The proprietors of the camp picture theatre had offended the fellows, who showed their displeasure by partially burning the building. One evening, to break the monotony, some of the men surreptitiously extracted a couple of casks of unwatered beer from the brigade canteen. They rolled the barrels some distance across the sand, and proceeded to enjoy themselves. The excited Greek barmen, early discovering the loss, turned out the guard. Following the tracks in the sand, they soon found the merrymakers, routed them, and recovered a little beer. The guard took their toll, and returned the balance to the outraged Greeks. A small Armenian general goods shop chose to over-charge, with the result that the vainly-expostulating merchant found his lean-to razed to the ground before his eyes.

Mac himself suffered from a severe overdose of C.B. So did his cobber Smoky. They had had the awful misfortune to be detected at an early hour one morning making their way to their lines. It had been sheer bad luck that had done it. If Smoky had not insisted on appropriating from the supply depot some "tinned cow" and a few small jars of beef extract, all would have gone well. Creaking boards

51

had started the trouble, and a conscientious sentry had put the tin hat on it. Ten days was the sentence—not that it mattered so much, for C.B. meant little beyond having to go out without passes by back ways—rather a nuisance if one were in a hurry for the train.

But it was the conscientious sentry which annoyed them. Why should the fool be so bally unreasonable as to report? They, the trooper and Smoky, were not so beastly particular when they did guard. In fact, such occasions offered unique opportunities for replenishing the private larders of their respective tents. New Zealand social theory held that one man was as good as another, so why should not they, as well as the officers, live upon the fat of the land, or such of it as could be got at Zeitoun Camp. Those were the days before army discipline was fully appreciated.

Other troubles were also theirs. C.B. was indeed a very minor ailment compared with their *piastreless* condition. The trip to Alexandria had absorbed all their available capital, earned and borrowed. Some coon, also, had stolen the trooper's washing from the line between the tents, and his wrathful mutterings against the miserable perpetrator of this horrible crime was awful to hear; but, privately, the trooper was keeping an eye open for someone else's washing. Both had aches in their left arms from the M.O.'s latest injection, and altogether they considered themselves much-abused, long-suffering soldiers.

Vague rumours floated round, some doubtless originating from that indispensable apparatus of every camp, the backyard wireless station. No great reliance could be placed upon such information, but occasionally statements based on much more stable foundations circulated. That a troop-train was standing in the siding at Palais de Koubbeh, and that there were several transports moored in Alexandria, was absolutely positive proof that the N.Z.M.R. were about to land in Asia Minor or to be at Constantinople in a week or two. Other proofs were not lacking—a super-abundance of staff officers in the vicinity, or confidences from the orderly room clerk. Then came the definite fact, and the wireless was temporarily idle.

It was a Wednesday night. The brigadier himself asked the brigade whether they would volunteer to go to Gallipoli as infantry.

Well, it was not too good leaving the horses; they would have preferred going into action with the "*prads*" but they didn't mind doing anything to get out of this Godforsaken country and into the real thing. So, all was business; grouses were forgotten and a new day dawned. Each in his own way set about squaring up his kit, his saddlery and his affairs generally.

Mac overhauled his with much care and thoughtful consideration. Into his base kit went those things which would come in handy in Constantinople. He had heard it was a cold place in winter-time, so therein went six complete suits of warm underclothing, and many superfluous comforts from his thoughtful mother. He knew she had put much work into many of these small knick-knacks, and valued them accordingly, though they were of little material benefit in this flaming spot. In another neat pile he had those articles which were absolutely essential for Gallipoli; but he was soon faced with the horrible reality that there was at least three times too much for his equipment.

He culled several times, the final combing causing much mental strain and strong will. Into a barley sack went his saddlery, with a reserve of many straps, buckles and horse-brushes, all collected at odd moments. Rifle, revolver, field-glasses, everything underwent a thorough overhaul. Ammunition was clipped and forced into the leather pouches of *bandoliers*, which equipment appeared neither to be meant for nor accustomed to such practical use.

Forty-eight hours after the first warning, the last night came. A subdued murmur arose from the camp. Some busied themselves with final preparations; some glided silently away from the zone of flickering candle-light, towards the horse-lines to give a parting pat to their faithful horses, a sad farewell for many; some joined the cheery crowd who were making the most of their last moments at the canteen; and others, less careless and more sober-minded, sought a few moments of sleep.

At eleven o'clock they fell in on their last parade in Egypt, though few regretted that. Nevertheless, when it came to the pinch, it was a little sad to leave the old camp, where, happily enough, they had passed six months of sun and sandstorm. A rough crowd they looked, these amateur infantrymen, overloaded with awkward, extemporized gear. They stood silent, for thoughts ran deep now that they were at last on the brink of the real thing, a moment towards which they had looked so long. The roll was called. Mac mentioned that he had left something, and slipped away to give the old mare a farewell stroke. Words of command echoed through the stillness, and soon the whole brigade was marching, as best it could, down the road towards the station. There were lusty cheers as they passed the guard tent from those whose turn had not yet come. The column turned to the left, and gradually the reverberating tread of heavily-laden men grew fainter in the distance.

So went the mounted brigade; and as they went to the north, following their infantry into the unknown, Mac and Smoky forgot their C.B., forgot their stiff arms and their *piastreless* condition—they thought only of the future.

CHAPTER 12

Gallipoli at Last

The sun had just risen when the train, a clattering collection of third-class cars, jangled laboriously over the low elevation on which Alexandria stands. With a series of nerve-racking spasms, it came to a halt on the waterfront, where lay several large transports absorbing men, horses and stores.

With some difficulty and many lurid epithets, the troopers slowly disengaged themselves from the unhealthy boxes, and gathered in sleepy groups to await developments, a thing they were in the habit of doing for long periods at a time. Mac and Smoky availed themselves of the first opportune moment, when all who mattered were engaged in calculations and scraps of paper, to disappear in the direction of a small buffet whence came a tempting rattle of crockery and an aroma of tea.

Here, even at this early hour, the good English ladies of Alexandria were dispensing refreshing tea and cakes to the soldiers.

Later they filed on board, and were taken, each unit to its own mess-deck, to deposit their gear. Mac's own troop had just completed the disintegration of themselves and their kit and the satisfactory stowage of it, when it was discovered that they were in the wrong part of the ship. Of course, that sort of thing was only to be expected, but Smoky was particularly annoyed, as he had succeeded in procuring the snuggest corner of the place. So, muttering and growling, they gathered up their goods and chattels, and shoved and groused along crowded alley-ways. Embarkations and disembarkations always were a severe trial of the temper.

They eventually got settled again, and soon divested themselves of unnecessary clothing and equipment. Then Mac and Smoky deemed it the most tactful course to seek a secluded corner of the boat deck, not infested by blustering non-coms, seeking fatigue parties. They proceeded to go to sleep in the shady security of the lee side of a lifeboat; but, as ill luck would have it, their own sergeant soon spotted them, and it was useless to pull his leg.

It was a loading fatigue, of course, and they were sent away along the waterfront to shove trucks about. They eventually selected one and brought it down alongside their ship. Black, greasy, heavy cooking apparatus it was, which had to be carried up the steep gangways and transported to the bowels of the ship.

During the rest of the day, they mostly slept in quiet corners of the ship.

Soon after dark they sailed. The vessel manoeuvred slowly through the breakwaters, and passed out on the calm waters of the Mediterranean. The low, blacker line of the Egyptian shore grew less distinct, and the numerous lights of the port came closer and closer together, faded into a dim halo and merged at length into the black sweep of the horizon. So passed Egypt from the sight of many; with the gurgling monotone of the propeller, they reeled off the knots of water which separated a past of careless happy-go-lucky days from a future of unfathomable depth.

There were no hammocks nor bunks on board the *Grantully Castle*. Either it was not considered necessary that soldiers should sleep or else, perhaps, that they were not at all particular. Anyhow there were worse places than hard decks to sleep on. Mac and Smoky scorned the fuggy atmosphere of the lower decks, and proceeded to select a breezy spot on the after boat-deck. They loosened the canvas cover of a lifeboat, levelled oars and other prominent obstacles, and disposed their scanty bedding to the best possible advantage on this uneven ground. The experiment was not altogether an unqualified success and minor disadvantages made themselves apparent during the passage of the night. The oars were rigid and uneven, and the breeze and the cold penetrated from both above and below. Still they stuck it out, and for the most part slept.

The following day fled by speedily and uneventfully. All gear was overhauled and guards were mounted; spare time was passed in gambling. Those who had money wanted to get rid of it. It was of no more value; in the future it counted for nothing, so large stakes were won and lost. Mac refrained from this indulgence, not that he was a conscientious objector, but, alas, he had no *piastres* wherewith to beguile the hours. His last two had been burst in one wild rapture on indigestible cake at the ship's canteen.

That night Mac was detailed for ship's guard. His duty it was to stand at the starboard quarter alongside a life-buoy, which he was to hurl at any fool of a trooper who unwittingly fell overboard. He was to report speedily of such affairs as submarines, fires and so forth.

During the long night watches, he forgot, more or less, all about his duty, and meditatively regarded the whirling wave as it seethed away into the darkness. All was silence, except for the mumble, mumble, mumble of the propellers. They were in the Aegean Archipelago and islands passed in an unbroken procession of indistinct shadows. Mac's thoughts were far away, and he was thinking of just such a night off Pelorus Sound, when a "Wake up, old sport! Time's up!" brought him suddenly to the present. He found Smoky had made a comfortable "possie" underneath two lifeboats and was sleeping soundly. He muttered only a few protesting groans on being shoved into his own share of the possie; and soon Mac had joined his cobber in the sound undisturbed slumber of an ordinary trooper.

The next day passed in much the same manner; but, alas, the night—Mac and Smoky were blusteringly ejected from their bivvie by an officious sergeant, who said that the poop boat-deck was holy ground reserved for machine-gunners and men on guard. So, they retired to the upper deck, and sought a spot whereon to lay their bones; but the ship was very full, and space limited. In an ill-considered moment they settled down partly under a seat, where passengers had sat in the palmy days of peace, and partly in an open gangway.

It proved an evil spot. Each changing guard trod on them, and retreated with awful blasphemy echoing in their ears. Then it chose to thunder, and rain fell in torrents. Not only from the skies, but also from the deck above it came in fountains, until the troopers were wretched in the extreme. There was no refuge whence to flee. Leaving their oil sheets and blankets meant only greater damp, so they stuck it out.

By daylight the rain had lessened, and the troopers, bedraggled and sleepy, disentangled themselves from the sodden blankets, and set about getting things in order. Smoky gathered up the wet clothes and surreptitiously made his way to the engine-room, where he selected a not too conspicuous steam main on which to hang them.

It was a damp grey morning. The vessel was steaming very slowly towards where appeared dimly through the mist a host of vessels of all descriptions, warships, transports, hospital ships and small craft. Ahead loomed the land, not very high, and indistinct in the rain.

At last, Gallipoli! The trooper regarded it suspiciously. It looked miserable, and he felt likewise. After the long, bright months in Egypt, the damp penetrated his bones, and he hadn't had breakfast. Anyhow, he supposed it wouldn't be so bad, and went off downstairs for a wash.

When Mac and Smoky, having breakfasted, disentangled themselves from the Bedlam of a troop-deck meal, and gained the upper air, they were in better humour to regard their surroundings from a philosophical, if not an appreciative, standpoint. The depressing drizzle had ceased, the clouds were breaking, and the shore, except for the mist-filled *nullahs* and the cloud-wrapped Asiatic hills, showed up more clearly in the morning light.

The *Grantully* had anchored about half a mile from the fort at Seddul Bahr, which with the castle and the village was shattered and forlorn. An untidy medley of tents, mules and stores of all description, covered the seaward slope and the beach to the left. Small craft passed rapidly to the shore from many French and British transports. Great men-o'-war, grey and cold, lay without sign of life; destroyers cruised slowly and meditatively, and pinnaces foamed along in energetic haste.

The two troopers watched the scene with interest. They were still very hazy as to the actual degree of the success of the landing, or really how far across the Peninsula the original force had progressed. The papers said everything had been wonderfully successful, but Mac was rather sceptical. At any rate, they were not wasting any time in pushing the mounted men in as infantry.

The future was obscure and uncertain; but, with a feeling of eerie anticipation, he felt the freshness of the dawn of a new mysterious life, when men met men in mortal fight, when the false standards of civilization went to the devil, and man was man. It was good to be alive; to be one of that brigade of fine hefty fellows on the edge of the great adventure, when they would join in the greatest sport on earth.

From across the misty uplands to the north-east, like the crushing of a cart over a gravelly road, came the rattle of musketry fire. Then, as the visibility increased, warships manoeuvred into position, and fired slowly and deliberately at unknown inland targets. Occasionally the troop-ship shook from the shattering crash of the *Queen Elizabeth's* guns. Reflecting was not one of the trooper's habitual occupations; but undoubtedly these first scenes and sounds of the real thing were occasions for thought.

A bugle-call for parade cut short further philosophising, and preparations for disembarkation found him faced with questions far more worthy of mental effort than un-trooper-like sentiments concerning what might or what might not occur in the future. The leading difficulty was, of course, to get twice the permitted amount of equipment into the kit, and some must be discarded. He had two blankets, and decided to dispose of the lighter, then, changing into a clean shirt, he threw away the old one. Everything was finally reduced to the absolute minimum, and packed as neatly as possible in the temporary kit.

★★★★★★

Cape Helles was not the destination of the Mounted Rifle Brigade. In mid-afternoon the *Grantully*, under slow steam, passed northwards along the coast thirteen miles, and dropped anchor again in the middle of another fleet of transports about two miles off Anzac. All traces of the morning gloom had gone; and, to the troopers, accustomed so long to the low, barren sand-dunes of Egypt, these high Gallipoli hills and islands, bathed in the glory of an Aegean evening, brought memories of other coast-lines, Cook Strait maybe, or the Great Barrier.

The fellows crowded along the landward rail, and, with or without glasses, endeavoured to discover battle-signs and the positions of our men.

There were across the steep green hillsides several great scars, where the scrub was withered and the bare earth showed; but surely our main line was over that high ridge, for reports stated that the army corps had penetrated several miles. The artillery was awakening to its evening activity, field guns could be seen firing, and shells bursting on high crests. Heavy shells, learned later to be those from the *Goeben* in the Dardanelles Channel, shrieked occasionally out of the unknown, and sent up great geysers of water near a four-funnelled cruiser to the right. A steady *staccato* of rifle fire floated faintly from the heights. (See *The Goeben & the Breslau: the Imperial German Navy in the Mediterranean, 1914—The Flight of the Goeben and Bresla*u by A. Berkeley Milne, Julian S. Corbett, W. L. Wyllie and Others; Leonaur, 2020.)

The evening shadows deepened to darkness; the stars shone brightly, and against them the land stood in a black, shapeless mass.

Many lights from the bivouacs on the seaward slope gleamed like a miniature Wellington across the water. War seemed difficult to reconcile with so serene and perfect a night.

Two destroyers came alongside, one on the port, the other on the starboard. Struggling with their unwieldy equipment, the troopers filed down the gangways on to them. Mac sat down by the engine-room manhole and listened to great and wonderful stories from the leading stoker of dashes up the Narrows, long patrols in winter storms, and thrilling times during the landing.

They spun away shorewards. The hills loomed blacker overhead and the dim *staccato* of rifle fire became a ceaseless rattle.

Spent bullets buzzed past and hit the water with a *"plop."* This was interesting, and, with a thrill of pleasure, Mac felt at last he was under hostile fire. For days—indeed, for months—he had been worried internally by a great doubt. Would he be a funk? He was in a frightful funk lest he should be one, and to him this was a matter of great concern, though he mentioned it to no one, not even to Smoky. He wondered whether his cobber was affected in the same way, but thought not, as he was so keen to get to the front. So, he had felt a little ashamed. Well, anyhow, now he was entering the danger zone, he experienced no abdominal sinking, such as one might expect under these circumstances. His mind was relieved; and, with the full joy of life, he turned with interest towards the steep hills.

Bells clanged below and the engines stopped and reversed, and, with a seething of water, the destroyer lost way. Out of the darkness loomed several unwieldy lighters, splendidly admiralled by a slip of a middy. They came alongside and the men swarmed aboard. The lighters moved lumberingly beachwards. From above, the firing grew loud, and a falling bullet wounded a man—the first casualty. Men stood silent, or spoke in subdued murmurs. The whole thing was weird, yet beautiful—the still glory of the night, the eerie, echoing rattle from above, and the flickering lights of the bivouacs.

They grounded at last alongside a stranded barge, crossed it, and, filing down a plank to the shore, gathered in ragged line along the beach to await orders. What was expected of them that night, none knew. A few of the earlier arrivals, not too fully occupied with work or sleep completely to ignore them, welcomed them warmly, and immediately launched into long-winded accounts of previous fighting. With an air of conscious superiority, they gave them hints and advice, and told vividly of trials, troubles and dangers. All this the newcomers accepted unchallenged and with deep respect.

The narrow beach, or those parts of it not occupied by great piles of stores, or limbers and water-carts, was a seething mass of humanity and mules. Few of the men spoke, beyond a welcoming "How do, cobber," or a "Glad you've come, mate." They appeared out of the darkness and passed into it again with an air of steady practical purpose. Ant-like, they passed in continual streams from barges to stacks of boxes, whose size rapidly increased.

At length the brigade filed off along the stony beach to the left, halted frequently, while stray bullets passed with a low whirr overhead

59

and out to sea; and turned finally up a deep ravine to the right.

On the steep, scrub-covered sides they were ordered to bivouac for the night. Things were not too comfortable, but that was no cause for complaint. Mac and Smoky forced themselves under a holly bush, enveloped themselves in their oil-sheets, and braced their feet against stems of shrubs to prevent their sliding down the fifty degree slope. There was no cessation of the firing, and, in this ravine each report reverberated from one clay cliff to another in ringing, resonant notes. There were no other signs or sounds of fighting—only this musical din coming from the starry vault above.

The trooper thought a terrific battle must be raging, and pitied the poor fellows in the trenches. He learned later it was just Abdul's normal method of spending the night when he had the wind up. These sounds were not disturbing, and soon the cobbers, for the first time, were asleep under fire.

CHAPTER 13
Mac Joins in the War

Mac's first morning at Anzac was one of deep interest. He regarded his surroundings rather more after the fashion of a Cook's tourist than of a soldier; or, maybe, he more closely resembled a schoolboy at his first circus. No time was wasted over a scratch breakfast—bully beef and biscuits were consumed more as a duty than a pleasure. Then, together with many others of equally inquiring frame of mind, he betook himself to the crest of the ridge which shut in the ravine on the north. The scene from there was indeed pleasing—a sapphire sea meeting a widely sweeping beach, a green, tree-dotted flat, and some scrub-covered hills, all sparkling with dew and bathed in the clear, tempered sunshine of an early summer morning. Mac's first impressions of Turkey left nothing to be desired, and there seemed promise of excellent bathing.

He gathered up shrapnel pellets and bits of shell casing, and with the true instinct of a globe-trotter, thought already of mementoes to take home. His tourist tendencies, however, soon evaporated, for he was sent round on a fatigue to the landing, whence he returned a sweating, blowing trooper, with a handleless, uncovered, paraffin tin of water. As he stumbled back along the stony beach an enemy battery opened fire without, it appeared, the Turks having precise knowledge of their target, or else their observation was inferior. To them, ignorance was bliss, just as the consistency with which they dropped salvos of four shells about two hundred yards out to sea, was bliss to Mac. Moreover, the paintbrush-like splash of the flying fragments demonstrated exactly what military instructions had been endeavouring to impress upon him for months concerning the field covered by a bursting shrapnel shell.

It had not been a great strain on the intellect of the enemy to deduce that the appearance of so many interested sightseers on the skyline indicated the presence of fresh troops in the *donga* below, and he consequently set about shelling it. Mac's regiment departed for the trenches at this juncture, and so missed the excitement. They kept along the shore for a short distance, then turned to the right, and started straight up the steep, narrow badly-graded paths towards the more or less flat summit, where they were to relieve an infantry battalion.

The sun was hot, and the way was steep, not to mention the weighty burden of equipment. The cool sea drew farther away as they soared gradually skywards, panting and perspiring. They reached their trenches at last, pushed themselves along ditches too narrow to take simultaneously both them and their gear, cast loving epithets at telephone wires which caught their rifles, and waited interminable times for the man ahead to move on. Towards midday, after dodging backwards and forwards, time and again, like a freight train in a railway yard, they collapsed at last in their appointed positions.

By evening Mac was thoroughly settled in his new home, and no longer did he regard his situation as being in the least unique. He reviewed the field of fire, studied the landscape, rather an extensive and interesting one; and had a few long-range shots at Turkish trenches. There was really no call for this, but it was rather amusing to be potting away, at last, at an enemy position.

His trench was not an exciting spot, separated, as it was, by a ravine from the enemy, and being only the protective flank of their own position.

The mounted men were soon accustomed to the new life, and in three days they might have been at it for ever. The days passed in a not unpleasant routine. The fresh, bright, beautiful dawns were slightly chilly, the early mornings were far from unpleasant, though the noonday hours were warm, and afflicted with flies and smells; but, beneath the shade of outstretched blankets and oil-sheets, the troopers whiled away the time, sleeping mostly, some writing and some playing cards. There was no reading material in those days.

The afternoon hours dragged drowsily past, until, with the lowering sun, they woke to prepare the evening meal, the largest of the day. Culinary operations were strictly limited by the short supply of water, so that meals were usually confined to bully-beef, biscuits, marmalade, bacon, or Maconochie. Both Colonials and Turks having completed their evening repast, the cool, clear evenings were spent by the former in sniping and artillery practice, and by the latter in expending wastefully large quantities of small arms ammunition against the opposite parapets.

Then, too, the troopers reassumed their clothing, most of which had been discarded during the day. As the gloaming deepened, the sniping ceased, but the Turks, ever mindful of the possibility of an attack, seldom throughout the night slackened their fire, which rose spasmodically to violent outbursts, probably in consequence of optical delusions on the part of a nervy follower of Mohammed, or, maybe, in response to horse-play on the part of the invaders. A Maori *haka* was sometimes responsible for the discharge of many cases of enemy ammunition.

During the hours of darkness many huddled forms lay in the bottom of Mac's trench, overlapping and cramped, but, nevertheless, peacefully sleeping. Here and there stood a sentry, his figure warmly cloaked and his face periodically lit by the glow from his pipe. Occasionally bullets hummed threateningly the length of the trench and these Mac regarded with deep respect, and addressed in words of wrath. The countless thousands which whistled crosswise over the trench, or else with a spurt of flame struck the sandy parapet, left him unmoved. The first half of his sentry-goes passed quickly enough, but the second dragged a bit, his thoughts being exhausted, and those beastly whirling enfilading bullets seeming to come more frequently.

At dawn all stood to, absorbed rum, of the liberally watered variety, exchanged experiences of the night, and smoked. Then the routine of the day began again, some dissolved once more into sleep, some remained on guard, and others went on the long weary journey for water.

The first week on Walker's Ridge passed fairly uneventfully, and by the end of it the garrison looked war-worn veterans. Water was very scarce, and a shave, much less a wash, altogether out of the question. In a moment of wild extravagance Mac had burst a couple of tablespoonfuls on cleaning his teeth. Towards the end of this week, being in support for twenty-four hours, they were able to go down to the beach for a bathe.

Never was bathing so much enjoyed, nor the sun-bath after it—it was just like old Maoriland again. There was always the *pop-pop-popping* on the hills above, the occasional thud of a spent bullet in the scrub, and the more or less methodical bursting of shrapnel shells somewhere along the shore; but all these circumstances had become so much part of the scene that the troopers were seldom perturbed. Sometimes a Turkish machine-gunner or sniper became a little too accurate or shrapnel fell a trifle too thickly on the beach to be comfortable, and were roundly cursed for their attentions.

On the night of their seventh day ashore, Smoky and Mac communed, and agreed that campaigning so far had not been particularly trying; that bully, biscuits, dirty water, and the same trenches were becoming over-monotonous, and that the time had already come when something ought to be done.

Their lust for more excitement was partly appeased that night. Old Abdul supplied the initiative, and later must have regretted it sorely.

Shortly after midnight, the usual nocturnal battle-sounds rose in a swift crescendo of bursting shells and rattling *staccato* of machine-gun fire, which echoed in weird music from cliff to cliff and across the ravines.

Mac—he was in a support trench—woke with a thrill to this grand din of battle, speedily assumed his *bandolier*, water-bottle and revolver, grasped his rifle, and trundled away up the sap after his disappearing cobbers.

They bundled up into the support of the main position, which was being attacked frontally by wave after wave of the enemy, who came on bravely, but were being mowed down in hundreds by machine and rifle fire. The defenders, in their eagerness, went out into the open to get a better field of fire, and to meet Abdul with the bayonet. Mac had rotten luck. His troop reinforced a flank position, where, no matter how strongly they used their wills, no Turk would venture. He waited and watched. In the gathering light of the dawn he could look more deeply into the scrub that shrouded vision beyond twenty-five yards, but nothing of interest revealed itself. He passed up ammunition and absorbed eagerly all tidings brought from the front line by the returning wounded.

As the sun rose, and the firing, instead of coming in the wild bursts, the lulls, and the wilder squalls of the earlier morning, decreased to a steady interchange of shots, Mac realised that the force of the attack was spent. With a deep sadness in his heart he emptied the breach of his rifle—the rifle which he had tended with great care and solicitude in anticipation of such an occasion as this.

He cursed gently and sadly as his troop filed sorrowfully back to their support trench, where, spitefully shelled with shrapnel, he set about the preparation of a belated breakfast for his section, two of whom had retired to possies to sleep, and the other to the beach for water.

CHAPTER 14

A Weary Day

Mac sat in the dust, his back against a bank, with his rifle leaning slantwise across him, and his equipment hanging awkwardly. Beside him sat Smoky, and both were melancholy. The sun beat strong in upon them, and the dust clung thickly to their perspiring bodies. The shady side of the wide communication trench was exposed to shrapnel, which the Turks had kept up more or less continually since the failure of their night attack. Against the opposite bank lay a body, half-covered by a blanket, and the *padre* was quietly removing the dead man's identification disc and the contents of his pockets. His two cobbers had gone on to the top to dig him a grave, and had both been wounded by shrapnel.

Mac and Smoky were sad. It was not the sorrow of grief, nor yet the thoughts that a speedy end might any time be theirs; but rather they were touched partly by the sight of the good old *padre* silently removing the soiled, time-worn articles from his pockets, small things which would be so greatly valued and revered by his people away in a sunny Wairarapa homestead, and partly the vision of a fine strapping, cheery fellow passing so rapidly from laughter to cold silence.

Thoughts such as these, deep and sincere as they were, cast but a passing shadow over their careless, happy natures. Friends of bush-whacking and shepherding days, camp mates of the past, and casual cobbers in Cairene escapades day after day went West; and always there came the momentary sadness, and, maybe, the remark, "Poor old Bill. They hooked him this morning. He was a good old sport." That was his requiem and, save for a few stray thoughts in the silent watches of the night, old Bill went unremembered.

The Turkish dead lay thick between the lines; but there was no knowing whether they had finally abandoned the attack. Their shelling continued, and the rifle fire indicated a nervous temperament. Consequently, the squadron still remained in reserve as near as possible to the firing line. Mac could see through a sap which ran to the edge of the precipice the beach and the cool, wonderfully cool-looking water. The few lucky beggars were splashing there, for practically every man was up in the firing-line. There were no troops to spare in those days—the line was but thinly held, and, if the Turks broke through anywhere, the whole position must be involved in disaster.

The day dragged slowly on to early afternoon. Then their troop was stirred into animation and excitement by the information that they and two other troops were to make a counter-attack "Light as possible, fifty rounds of ammunition only. . . First and second trenches . . . some machine guns and a few Turks. . . Clear them out and come back," were the orders.

They filed silently and with set faces to their assembly positions. They were in for something serious. They had all seen the waves of advancing Turks in the early morning dissolve away. Mac thought he didn't mind how soon peace was declared, and felt a bit tired of the war, but, still, here was their first real, live chance. A heavy covering fire had been opened all round the Anzac lines, and the enemy replied with equal force. His troop slipped over the parapet, and lay, awaiting the word, among the many dead, Turkish and Australasian, of last night, and of three weeks earlier.

Minutes passed slowly, five, ten, twenty, thirty—what on earth did this mean? The sun blazed fiercely on the flattened figures, the smell was awful, and the fire slackened not a bit. Mac had examined his breech a dozen times, adjusted and readjusted his ammunition to facilitate its easy handling, and had made certain several times of the firmness of his bayonet. He had thrown away his bayonet scabbard. It was long and might trip him up. If he came back, he could recover it; if he didn't—it wouldn't matter. He had heard it said that waiting was the worst time of all, and he longed to be off, even into that hail of bullets which whizzed low over his head.

More minutes marched funereally by, and then he heard in the trench behind the sound of voices, and an order passed along the line to clamber back into the trench. Surely there was some mistake, thought Mac, but no, it was repeated, and they wormed themselves back over the parapet, gathered hazily that the attack had been deemed inadvisable, and sauntered tiredly back to their old place in the communication sap. Talking it over later. Smoky and the trooper came to the conclusion that the cancelling of the attack was the best thing that had ever happened for them. Theirs would have been the fate of the enemy in their shattered attacks of the previous night, though, having made up their minds to it, and stood the forty-five minutes' strain of waiting, it had seemed a bit tough not to be repaid with a whack at the Turks.

The long hot day drew at length to a close. The setting of the sun amidst the islands was full of wild beauty. The airy pinnacles of Samothrace and the wild hills of Imbros, scarred and parched, stood silhouetted against a glorious background of wonderful colouring, high tones and low tones, an idealised Turner canvas. Out to the sinking sun stretched a golden path, while to the right and to the left lay untroubled leagues of blue. The gloaming slowly enveloped the horizon to the north and south, the shining path of light broadened and burnished, as the sun rested a moment, then disappeared, while the island grew darker against the riot of deep colouring.

Resting on a clay ledge on the edge of the cliff which rose precipitously to a height of 600 feet a few hundred yards from the shore, Mac and Smoky drank in the glory of these rare moments. Both sides were tired, the Turks weary of the carnage and their failure, and the invaders of the hot, waterless hours of waiting, but conscious of their successful defence and increased security.

They discussed the events of the day, the prospect of a swim on the morrow, and, as always, of the long shandies, the ham and eggs, and the apple pie which they would have on that great occasion when they returned once more to New Zealand. Yes, a bush *whare* was all that Smoky would want for the rest of his life, a possie where he could eat and drink and sleep just as much as he wished. He aspired also to brands of tobacco other than those the army thought suitable to his taste.

These pleasant anticipations of the future were abruptly cut short by the order, "Stand to." From Mac's point of view this was quite an unnecessary proceeding, involving much inconvenience and discomfort, and, in the early morning hours, loss of valuable sleep. Still, these things had to be put up with, and "stand to" could be profitably spent cleaning rifles and other gear. The issue of rum, when not stopped by the higher command or absorbed by the A.S.C. and quartermasters, was occasionally a relieving and pleasant interlude about this time.

"Stand to" ended, they composed themselves to sleep where they were, which was still in the same communication trench in reserve. The trench was five feet in width—in favourable spots it may have been six—and the bottom was deep in dust, which, to a certain extent, moderated the sharpness of ammunition pouches in the middle of one's back. From the heaps of piled-up spoil above came irregular avalanches of dust and dirt, and due care had to be taken to prevent it getting in one's ears, eyes, nose and mouth. Still, notwithstanding these minor discomforts, Mac had managed to get about an hour's sleep before matters became trying.

The artillery were immediately responsible for it all—the artillery, for which, in spare moments from the firing line, they had dug this communication trench and gun-pits beyond, and had even dragged the pieces up. Now, at this infernal hour, they chose to bring their ammunition up. Trains of mules arrived, halted close alongside where Mac lay huddled against the bank, moved at right angles across the sap, were relieved of their burdens and departed again, led by their shadowy Indian muleteers.

Mac was hardened to being walked on by men, but mules laden with eighteen-pounder shell...... Badly pinched and deeply angered, he stuck it for a while. There was nothing to be gained by swearing, for the mules and the Indians were equally indifferent. More mules were followed by still more mules, which, as they turned, trampled on him severely. Heavy hoofs were placed squarely on his shrinking person, and he had at length to give them best.

There was nowhere else to go, so, leaning against the wall, he awaited brighter moments. Often, he cursed wrathfully, occasionally he smoked. This ruthless violation of his valuable hours of sleep was a crime he would not readily forgive the artillery, and he wished their bally guns had been shoved somewhere else. The mules came and went for hours, occasional suspensions of their comings and goings only creating in his breast false hopes.

Towards dawn he slept once more, only to be aroused again for the purpose of swinging up towards the front line for support. No attack came, and now, the sun rising above the eastern hills, he and his troop trailed wearily back to their own bivouacs. His section four discussed breakfast, the contents and limited possibilities of the larder, the disappearance of firewood, which had been carried off by some person during their absence, and the absolute non-existence of water.

"Breakfast be blowed!" said Mac. He crawled into his niche in the side of the trench, covered himself in his grey blankets, head included, for protection from flies, left breakfast worries to the others, and passed into the deep slumber of the utterly weary.

CHAPTER 15

Mac is Sleepy

Mac's luck was out. He had had practically no sleep the night previous, or, for that matter, for the two nights before that again, and he was not going to get any chance to make it up now. A distant echo of his name from somewhere up the sap brought a swift awakening. It was an evil omen, portending the worst fatigue. He decided to follow the lazy course of action, namely, to avoid it if possible.

"Mac! Where in the devil are you? Mac! Mac!"

The exhorting voice of the corporal came nearer; but the trooper decided he was a heavy sleeper and knew, moreover, that his whole form was well shielded by his grey blanket. As usual though, all this was futile, and no effort of will could persuade the corporal to pass unmolested his shrouded form. The blanket was pulled from over his face, and, with a slap on the thigh and "Come on, Mac!" shouted down to him, he could hardly, with decency, pretend to be asleep any longer. He carried the thing to rather too flourishing a finish, awakened violently with a suspicious suddenness, and blinked rapidly at the corporal, "Oh! Rations you're after. All right. I'll dodge away down after them. You might give a feller a chance to sleep though." He knew well it was about his turn to wander away down the hill for rations, but a fellow was sorely tempted to put off the evil moment to the last, when, utterly weary, he was enjoying some rare hours of settled sleep.

Mac trudged wearily away down the ridge, at times almost letting his legs run away with him on the steep paths. At the depot, he persuaded the water-guard to let him fill his water-bottle, and then, while the Quarters calculated together, he drowsed in the shade of a bank. For some time, the Quarters chewed the ends of their pencils, studied note-books and tapped boxes. Then they retired in the direction of a comfortable service corps dug-out, whence issued spirals of blue smoke and odours of rum.

By and by they emerged, and all struggled into activity again. Some of the fatigue party had disappeared though, for they were not often so close to the beach. Still, the Quarter was not worried, for he knew all would return *anon*, each to lump his load up the track. Mac had been too sleepy to wander off for a bathe, though, as a matter of fact, he had been endeavouring for the last twenty minutes before the Quarter's return to summon up sufficient energy to follow his cobbers' example. Still, boxes of biscuits would be their portion, while, getting in early, he would be able to secure easy freight, flitches of bacon or the like.

He shouldered his load and set off homewards. He rested often for the first half of the journey, but then, pulling himself together, plugged steadily upwards. Towards the summit, where the track ran up a razor-back, his progress was hastened by the Turkish artillery on the "W" Hills. He deposited his bacon at the Quarter's bivvie, and wandered down the sap to his ledge under the wall. Delving into a battered biscuit tin, he produced some characterless dried flour tiles, a tin of bully and a tin of apricot, the choicest of Deakin.

His three cobbers, who were the only other inhabitants of this section of the sap, had breakfasted, and now lay, like three mummies, on their respective ledges. This trench was merely the wing of a sector, and was not directly opposed to an enemy trench. Here it was the privilege of his section to make its headquarters every third day, when it was their additional privilege to do the ration and water fatigues, to furnish sapping and burying parties, sentries and guards, and such other toilers as might be necessary; while occasionally, with great luck and better management, an hour or two on the beach might be worked.

Here, with his back against a traverse, Mac set about his repast. He devoured half a tin of bully. That was his limit, no matter how hungry he was, for he was aware by experience of the effects of overmuch bully. He shied the remainder over the parapet, and promptly set about his second and last course. The flies were fonder than he of Deakin's apricot, and he had to be circumspect to dodge them successfully. He knew too well their other sources of food supply—and was not over keen on swallowing any, nor of having them beating him for his jam, Deakin's though it was.

With some difficulty he broke the bullet-proof biscuits into mouthful sizes, grasped the tin of jam between his knees with his hand over it, and dipping each bit first into the jam, popped it into his mouth. Mac had good teeth, but, all the same, it took many long minutes of hard jaw work to get on the outside of a biscuit and a half. This, he had calculated, was as much dry tack as his daily ration of dirty water could comfortably counterbalance.

He then set about putting his domestic affairs in order—tidying up his kit and his bivvie, overhauling the larder, shaking his dusty blankets and the like. He surveyed his weather-beaten countenance in a broken triangle of glass. "What-o, mother, that you should see me now!" and he winked whimsically at himself. A fortnight's black beard formed a dark halo round his features, plenty of dust from the heaps of earth above stuck in his hair, and he was already a bit thinner than in Egyptian days. At the present moment a pair of ragged shorts, hanging insecurely about his middle, was his only garment. The rest of his body was, like his face, tanned and dusty.

He now performed to the full such toilet as was possible in his present quarters. He rubbed himself vigorously with a towel, cleaned his teeth with about two dessert-spoonfuls of water, and brushed his hair. He gave his rifle a few runs through and a dust, and restored round the bolt a careful wrapping of cloth. This completed the setting of his house in order.

A corporal sang out from up the sap that the troop was to be ready for the front line at one o'clock, so Mac roughly, but good-naturedly, tumbled his cobbers off their ledges and admonished them to turn to and prepare.

The next half-hour was spent in getting ready, dressing, having some lunch, which varied not from the earlier repast, and attaching gear. They looked a shabby mob, with their equipment slung round them and their clothing adapted to individual taste. As mounted men put in suddenly to reinforce the foot, their equipment was not all it might have been for trench warfare; but they had come to work and not to a beauty show.

They filed away up the dusty, sun-scorched sap, through narrow communication trenches, bringing forth disgusted curses from the dwellers therein, whose cooking and living arrangements were suspended during their passage; and settled finally in an advanced sap leading out towards the enemy lines. It was deep and narrow and had no conveniences either for comfort or fighting. The afternoon drowsed slowly past, a spell of sapping at the sap-head occasionally breaking the monotony.

With sundown, both sides revived for the evening activity, a meal, and preparations for the night. The Turks, since their heavy but futile attacks of two nights previous, had not returned into that placidity which betokened cessation of evil intentions. There was an erratic nervousness of fire; instructions were that an attack would eventuate during the night, and that no one was to sleep.

Just about sunset, word floated up from behind that a white flag was approaching, but it was some time before it and several attendant Turks appeared through the scrub about a chain to the right. Too many accompanied the flag, but nearer approach being severely discouraged they retired speedily again into the scrub. A few minutes later, the flag returned, this time direct towards the sap-head, and now the colonel, armed with German and Turkish vocabularies, was there to welcome it. They halted about twenty yards away, and a rather fruitless conversation followed. The Turks jabbered excitedly a meaningless chorus, to which the colonel, full of importance and dignity, replied with deliberate and forceful phrases of alleged Turkish and German, fluttering the while through the vocabularies and prompted and admired on all sides by an audience of officers and men.

The Turks were unimpressed, and gabbled on. Now arrived the right man, the interpreter—all would be well. But, alas, he was so nervous and alarmed at being thrust on the parapet that the conversation profited little by his presence! All that could be impressed upon the flag-bearers was that they were to return home as speedily as possible, which course they wisely adopted, and immediately a burst of firing broke out along both lines. This calmed as rapidly as it had begun, and the troopers, chuckling over the comical scene of the colonel airing his German and Turkish, drank their rum and settled down to the long vigil.

A glorious night it was, still and starry, and sound travelled far. But it was very weary, standing hour after hour waiting for the attack. From the sap-head came the steady tapping of the picks and occasionally the sound of muffled voices. Water was very scarce, but the drowsiness which crept over the trooper was the worst of his troubles. Attack or no attack, he could not keep awake. Every few seconds he fell asleep, his knees kinked under him, and he was once more awake. This grew monotonous, but there was no stopping it. His interest was caught at times by the jabbering of assembling Turks in the hollow just over the scrub-covered rise.

Searchlight beams had been scouring the hills to the north, and one was suddenly thrown on no man's land. Batteries ashore and destroyers opened fire. Shells whirred up from below, screamed overhead and burst beyond the rise. The jabbering rose into an impassioned chanting to *Allah*. The searchlight switched off, the shells fell less frequently, the Oriental *obligato* fell away in a diminuendo of pathetic cries and a *staccato* of terrified jabbering. Mac's knees again kinked frequently.

In his state of alternate consciousness, the minutes dragged wearily, he lost all count of time, and the whole business merged into a vivid distorted dream. The drama was repeated, the mutterings of

71

the assembling Turks, the long-searching beam coming up from the sea, the sudden tearing and crashing of the artillery, and the agonised howlings of the enemy. Then came another period of quiet and deep drowsiness.

There may have been a third enactment, though on this point Mac has always been hazy. At any rate, in due course came the dawn. The sky brightened behind the Turkish lines, the searchlights faded away, and gradually the spasmodic rifle fire of the night fell to occasional single shots along the line. "Stand to" laboured by on leaden wings. A single sentry was posted at the sap-head; then, in awkward attitudes and angles, like the corpses on the ground above, they fell asleep in the bottom of their sap.

CHAPTER 16

Various Misfortunes

Mac, minus most of his clothing, squatted on a heap of rubble, keenly following through his glasses, naval tactics on the sea below. One favourable point about Anzac was that, if one was bored with everything else, there was always plenty to look at, especially with a good pair of glasses. This morning, coming out on to the little flat top behind his position, he discovered all the shipping in a turmoil. The whole fleet of twenty or more transports was going helter-skelter for Imbros harbour, the winches of a few laggards still rattled as they laboured with their anchors, cruisers patrolled uneasily up and down, fleet-sweepers moved about nowhere in particular, while destroyers dashed round in wide circles, leaving behind them trails of heavy black smoke and foaming white water. Only a couple of white hospital-ships remained undisturbed.

"Submarines—damn them!" thought Mac. This was a new and unpleasant development and not to his liking at all. He descried through the haze the anchorage at Cape Helles, and noted that the vessels there—among them a huge four-funnelled Atlantic liner—were also making off.

Towards evening all transports had disappeared, and cruisers and destroyers resumed a leisurely patrol.

That was Saturday. In the early light of next morning, while the mist-wraiths still clung to the hills and filled the *dongas*, Mac was disturbed in his breakfast preparations by the sound of a heavier cannonade than usual to the south. Going to an observation post he saw a battleship aground off Gaba Tepe Point. The morning mists had just revealed her, and now she was emptying her broadsides in rapid succession up the great valley below Kilid Bahr. Another battleship was right alongside attempting, apparently, to push her off.

White smoke from many bursting Turkish shells mingled with the heavy black pall from the discharging broadsides. The bombardment continued for some time, and Mac at length returned to his neglected breakfast preparations, his going hastened by the fact that, carelessly exposing his head, he had attracted the attentions of a sniper. When he looked later, both men-o'-war were some distance away steaming west.

He learned afterwards that the *Albion*, in taking up her position on the southern flank, had grounded in the mist, and that the *Canopus* had come to her assistance, attempting, without success, to get her off. The *Albion* lightened herself by emptying her magazines through her broadsides, and was finally towed off.

★★★★★★

Then came the armistice, a day of interest and amusement, and of grim, unpleasant work.

For almost a month, in no man's land, attack after attack had dwindled away to nothing and there, five days before, Turkish losses had been especially heavy. The enemy took the initiative in the matter, and white flag negotiations proceeded on several occasions.

Later, a gorgeously apparelled Turkish staff officer came across and was taken blindfolded to headquarters, where an armistice for internment purposes was agreed upon. Very considerate it was of Abdul to put the proposition, Mac thought, for the condition of the atmosphere in the neighbourhood was not conducive to his peace of mind, nor did it improve his inclination to eat to know that those flies which nothing could keep out of his food, had come from ——. And his internals would squirm at the thought.

A peculiar quietness had marked the passage of the night, and with the vanishing of the mists a strange silence filled the air. Since the landing nearly a month back, the continuous music of rifle fire, with its echoes and re-echoes among the nullahs and cliffs, had scarcely ever ceased. And now, from opposing parapets, cautious heads began to appear, Red Cross and Red Crescent flags were brought into the open. Large burying parties followed, and soon thousands of Cornstalks and Mussulmans were burying each others' dead. Thousands lined the parapets, scanning those acres of which they had had before but wily glances, or had scurried over in the wave of an attack. No one was going to miss the show. The cove was deserted, and the infantryman and the Service Corps man stood boldly side by side on the parapet.

Of the work itself little can be said. Mac was on duty in the first line, and was not allowed to leave it to investigate the secrets of no man's land, but he knew well enough of the huddled figures lying in clusters in that green scrub, which hid much. But in parts the scrub had been worn from the earth by the constant ripping of the bullets. There, partly shielded by withering branches lay withering bodies, mostly in strange postures, sometimes one above the other with rusting rifles, discarded equipment, and odd bits of wire. Often scraps of torn cloth clung to the jagged stems of shattered shrubs, and all was a scene of desolation unutterable.

So numerous were the dead that all day long the burying went on. Some of the workers, resting from their labours, attempted conversation with the Turkish parties, but ignorance of each others' language proved a difficulty. Still they smiled and gesticulated and exchanged cigarettes.

Towards the middle of the afternoon, parties finished their work and returned, no man's land became gradually untenanted, the curious were satisfied, and melted from the parapets, a sudden heat shower damping their ardour, and gradually the old scene came back. About four the white flags with their red emblems disappeared and every one retired discreetly into his trench. Soon a stray shot rang out, and the armistice was over. Snipers were at their old dodges, and later in the evening Mac's section received for some time the attentions of an enemy mountain gun, which was new to this part of the line.

The following day brought a tragedy which sank deep into Mac's heart.

Out on the left flank, near where the *Albion* had been ashore a few mornings back, a man-o'-war had always lain since the days of the landing. There had been some anxiety certainly on account of the submarine excitement the other day; but now, slow, lazy movements on the part of the destroyers and the reoccupation of old anchorages by the cruisers, indicated that naval peace of mind was once more restored. H.M.S. *Triumph* had anchored soon after daybreak on the southern flank.

Now, at midday, came the shout, "*Triumph's* been torpedoed." Mac jumped on his fire-step, and, looking down the trench, saw beyond it sure enough the poor old *Triumph* with a heavy list towards him. Some of the fellows had seen the torpedo strike her right amidships, and a great column of water rise high in the air and fall on her decks. From all directions destroyers, mine-sweepers and pinnaces were concentrating on the doomed vessel. Two destroyers had run their bows alongside her hull, and her crew was swarming off. Her decks grew steeper, but some of the crew seemed to be sticking to their guns to the last in the after turrets. Mac could not discover whether these shots were directed against the submarine or whether they were but the last farewell of the old battleship. Fifteen minutes from the moment she was struck, her decks lay almost at right angles to the water, then the movement quickening, she turned bottom upward, only her red keel, propellers and rudder showing to the troubled troopers who sadly watched the demise of the famous old ship.

A quarter of an hour longer she floated, sinking lower and lower, then, with an easy motion, she slid away from sight. For a few minutes a maelstrom of white, surging water foamed and spurted, then, sadly and slowly, the host of small craft which had rushed to the rescue made again for their stations. Destroyers manoeuvred in vain search of the submarine, while battleships and cruisers in a haze of smoke disappeared beyond the horizon. Only a few bright tins, some boards, and a patch of oil marked the spot on the peaceful, azure sea, where, an hour before, a fine old ship, and fifty of her crew, had gone to their doom.

The troopers ate their lunch in stony silence. It seemed they had lost an old friend.

Still, in going about the afternoon's work, they soon forgot their sadness. They had been a fortnight in these trenches, and now they were to be relieved by the Light Horse. It was good getting out after a fortnight there, but it was a darned nuisance moving. When Mac had all his gear up, there was not much of himself left in view. Valise, *bandolier*, rifle, revolver, glasses, water-bottle, extra ammunition, cooking utensils, haversack, a stove, the day's rations, a bundle of fire-wood, and half a dozen odds and ends had to find space about his person; the Q.M.S., too, usually had something to add to this load.

A heavy summer shower did not improve matters, and made the descent of the steep clay paths one of speed rather than elegance. Once started with so heavy a load, it was impossible to pull up. So, the descent of his regiment that afternoon from the plateau above was a weird and wonderful sight, and resembled nothing more than a mixed avalanche of perspiring troopers, mud and gear.

They took up their new abode on a steep northerly slope above the sea. Instructions were that all habitations were to be made shrapnel proof, but this was a matter of difficulty on so steep a face. Night-fall found Mac and his section with an awninged platform, six feet square and three feet high and partially walled, but far from shrapnel proof and never likely to be. They were not inclined to meet trouble half-way, so each disposed his equipment in its rightful spot. The four partook heartily of a most sociable evening meal, and then wandered off for a good long bathe in the pleasantly cool water of the Aegean.

★★★★★★

The bivouac on the steep slope north of Anzac Cove was hardly the safest, and domestic life there was not the most unruffled. Just when five more seconds would have seen the bacon done to a T, the whistle of the look-out up above would go. That meant that the Turkish battery on the W Hills had delivered itself of a missile, which might, or might not, be directed at this bivouac.

Then Mac would find himself in a dilemma. Would he trust to luck that the shell was not for him, and save the bacon, or would he crouch for safety under the protection wall? More often the bacon had the benefit of the decision for meal-time was Abdul's favourite hour for action, and, if Mac took heed of every warning, the section would never get through its meals. He knew that the warning whistle gave him seventeen seconds before the arrival of the shell, and, if he waited for the sound of the discharge, he had about four seconds left.

Still they didn't worry much until, after a few opening rounds, Abdul's practice got too good and there was no mistaking his malevolent attentions. Mac, if he were not near his own bivouac, would dive into the nearest one, irrespective of owner, and seek its leeward corners. A few seconds of quiet waiting while he exchanged the time of day with his host; then the burst, the singing whistle of the fragments, the whirr of the nose-cap, and the *fut—fut—fut* as the pieces came to earth. Then, if another whistle had not sounded, he would thank his host and proceed on his way.

Often would come the cry of "Stretcher-bearer," and the M.O. would hurry up the steep slope to someone who had been hit.

Mac lost his sergeant, a real fine fellow, one morning, while he was serving out rations. The whole regiment was grieved. For the rest of the day his body, shrouded in his grey blanket, lay on a stretcher in his bivouac with as much calm and holy dignity as any royal monarch lying in state.

Soon after dusk, for the little cemetery was under direct machine-gun fire during the day, the regiment gathered, bareheaded and silent, to bury its comrade. Six of the dead soldier's friends lifted the bier, and bore it tenderly down the steep slope and over the bridge across the sap. The regiment followed and gathered round the open grave.

It was given to few on the Peninsula to be buried thus. Many still lie where they fell on those Gallipoli hills; some are graced with shallow graves, scratched hastily under fire, among the torn and tattered scrub, while others, with fire-bars and blanket and with a few parting words, have been plunged into the blue Aegean.

On the little sandy point on the north of Anzac Cove is one small graveyard, where, when Mac knew it, were fifty or sixty graves. In the daytime it was shell swept and subject to direct rifle fire, but at night came shadowy figures which passed to and fro from the beach bringing neat stones and round boulders for picturesque and permanent adornment of a cobber's grave. Or maybe there would be some diggers at work, or a burying-party.

Tonight, in the peaceful calm of that summer evening, when not a ripple lapped on the stony beach, when the only indication of war was the music of the firing high above and the occasional whistle of a spent bullet overhead, the good old *padre*, in clear, low tones, went through the sergeant's burial service. The rites were finished, and the silent troopers moved away into the darkness as quietly as they had come, while the *padre* started the service anew among another group of silent, waiting figures.

And so, the summer passed over that little burial-ground. In the daytime, the scorching sun blazed over the crude crosses and whitened stones, and the shells shrieked by, while in the dark coolness of the night shadowy figures brought the day's toll silently and reverently to its resting place. (See also *On the Anzac Trail* by "Anzac" The experiences of a New Zealand soldier in Egypt and Gallipoli during the Great War; Leonaur, 2010.)

CHAPTER 7
An Outpost Affair

Fortunately for the regiment, most of the daylight hours during the short stay in the present bivouac were spent away on working-parties or in support to some section of the front line. They usually returned in the evening to find fresh holes in their oil-sheets and shrapnel pellets on their floors. Still, they often had a good night's sleep, and always a fine bathe in the morning.

While lodged on this slope, Mac and his squadron became involved in an engagement which kept them fully occupied for three days. One Friday evening at dusk they moved northwards along the beach to the farthest outpost. Inland from here about half a mile on a high ridge the Turks had commenced the formation of an outpost. About nine o'clock this was attacked and easily captured. Then the squadron commenced digging in, and, by dawn, with small loss, had dug a fairly satisfactory semi-circular position, facing over ravines, beyond which were higher hills.

The Turks were expected to counterattack, but contented themselves by sniping from all sides, which considerably impeded the work of consolidation. Mac and his section toiled and sweated all day, and, in the late afternoon, connected their section of trench with those on the right and left. Water had run dry, no communication could be had with the rear, the sun blazed down, with withering heat, and altogether Mac had known of pleasanter spots to spend a summer's day. In the afternoon, too, the Turks added shrapnel to their missiles.

About ten o'clock at night another squadron appeared for their relief, and Mac, with keen anticipations of a drink, a bathe and a sleep, speedily stumbled off through the scrub after his cobbers. Their line of march lay the length of a long ridge through enemy country, and on this ridge one of the destroyers protecting the flank chose this inopportune moment to cast her attention and her searchlight. Each time it caught him in its brilliant glare on the sky-line, Mac crashed down into the nearest shrub, prickly holly, arbutus or stunted oak, and cursed lowly to himself till the beam lifted. Progressing spasmodically when the beam was directed elsewhere, they reached the outpost, then stumbled wearily back along the beach, ate and bathed and turned in for a real long sleep.

They were to have no such luck. They had only just settled down when word came back that the enemy had closed over the ridge along which they had returned, and that the squadron in the new outpost was cut off. The only remaining squadron was sent out at once to their relief, but the Turks being in too great strength, it could do nothing. So, Mac's squadron, tired as they were, dodged away out again to another hard day's work in the blazing sun. It was now daylight, and certain spots had to be crossed by each man singly at a run, while the close attention of a Turkish machine-gun at long range lent wings to their feet.

With his head down and his teeth clenched, Mac would bolt full-speed across these open spaces. *Tut—tut—tut* would echo from the hills, then a whinging past his ears or a spurt of dust in too close proximity, and he would redouble his pace. The shelter of the bank on the farther side gained, he would turn to laugh at the expressions, whimsical, serious as death, or thoroughly amused, of his cobbers as they rapidly paced their hundred yards.

Arrived in a ravine which cut the ridge, they found the Turks in a position too strong to be attacked in daylight by so small a force. Eventually it was decided to await nightfall and strong reinforcements before attempting to force a passage through the Turkish lines to the beleaguered garrison of the outpost. They gathered in shady corners of the dried water-course, and yarned and smoked the long hot hours away. Shrapnel came screaming across the scrub in the afternoon, but spent itself harmlessly in desert spots.

It was decided that the outpost was too isolated a position to hold, and that, after nightfall, the enemy, who had entrenched, should be forced back, the besieged with their wounded withdrawn, and a retreat made to the old position. This was all successfully carried out. Mac took his fortunes with a covering party on the right flank. He could follow little of what was taking place up at the outpost itself. There was a good deal of rifle-fire and bombing, and a certain amount of shell-fire, whose great white flashes lit up the wild ravine in fleeting visions of weird beauty.

At midnight the order for retreat found Mac almost asleep, for he was very weary from long wakefulness. They passed silently down the valley, being apparently the last to go. The Turks were following the retirement, for they were chanting their weird invocations to *Allah* not very far distant.

At the foot of the ravine, near the ruins of a solitary fisherman's hut, he and half a dozen others were instructed to take up a position and to stick to it till the last. He expected that, when the Turks emerged from the dried-up watercourse, there would be some fun, but, though their cries to *Allah* floated down the ravine, along with some indiscriminate firing, they themselves did not choose to come. During the long wait here, the *padre*, heedless of danger from spattering bullets, which flicked fire when they struck the dust, and despite the dysentery which racked his frame, and the long days and nights without sleep, went right along the scattered exposed firing line, taking cheese, biscuits and water to the weary, thirsty troopers. Wherever they went in action there was their quiet old *padre*, always working among the wounded, and, if these lacked, he would join in some other good work, bringing up water and provisions, or the like.

The Turks had attacked heavily the summit of a ridge about one hundred yards to Mac's right, and here he was sent now to bring in wounded, one of whom three of them were instructed to carry round to Anzac Cove. It was a long and weary journey, stumbling over scrubby hillocks and then away along the stony beach. This bad going in the dark was pretty rough on the wounded man, but, like most in his condition, he stuck it splendidly, and was deeply grieved he was such a burden to his cobbers.

At length they reached the dressing-station at the cove, and placed him on a table in a room with sandbag walls. Several medical men examined the wound and spoke technically thereon. The stretcher-party asked anxiously after his condition, and sought tidings also of cobbers who had been brought back earlier. Then they set off for the firing-line once more.

The third dawn in this outpost affair was now lighting the eastern sky, beyond the hills where the night's fighting had taken place. Half-way back near the poppy-patch, one glorious riot of red summer flowers, they met their regiment returning. They had done their work, the Turks had ceased attacking and the weary regiment which had been kept busy the long, hot days in this outpost skirmish had been relieved. The tired troopers trailed homewards, carelessly tramping the dewy wild poppy heads on their way. A bathe and a drink, and then a long, long sleep.

The three days' skirmish had been an interesting little engagement. Mac thought that the establishment of an outpost so far beyond the Anzac territory had been undertaken rather too lightly. The cutting off of the garrison thirty hours from the time of capture, the relief of the besieged twenty-four hours later and the subsequent retreat were actions which had brought many anxious moments, plenty of hard work in the blazing sun, and the lives of some fine officers and men. The Turks, too, had suffered many casualties. The only tactical result of the operation was that the enemy chose to make the outpost of contention a strong, almost impregnable position, which was captured three months later only by a ruse and hard fighting.

Altogether it had been a pleasant scrap in the open, and Mac was not dissatisfied that he had gone through the experience. Anyhow as, profoundly and delightfully weary, he lay down on the hard clay floor of his bivouac, he felt a satisfied contentment with life.

★★★★★★

It was late that afternoon—Monday—when the troopers awoke and set about preparing a meal as sumptuous as the limited larder permitted. Since Friday only odd nibbles of bully and biscuit had passed into their internals.

That evening they cursed the Turks in free bush fashion for committing an act of a kind to which they usually rose superior. Facing the bivouac on the steep cliff below the disputed outpost, lay two stark white bodies. The enemy had apparently stripped the dead, of whom there were nine left in the outpost, and had flung the bodies over the cliff. The regiment was infuriated with this treatment of its dead, and vowed vengeance. Next morning a destroyer, with a few well-directed shots, blew up the bodies, and gradually the deed was forgotten.

Owing to the casualties from shell-fire on this slope, the following day was spent in moving to a new situation, not so pleasant as the last, and shut away in a ravine, but safer from shell-fire. Here all toiled solidly for two days, terracing a steep clay slope and making new homes.

And here for some days with the regiment the normal routine life of the Gallipoli summer campaign ran smoothly. The days were spent on road-work or on big communication saps, and at night, more often than not, there were sapping fatigues in the front firing line, squadron supports, heavy pieces of artillery to haul to their emplacement, and the like.

At most times there was work, but occasionally there were spare hours, when Mac and Smoky, with their towels and toothbrushes, would wander down to the beach for a morning of sea and sun-bathing. They would remove what few clothes they wore and take to the water. Only a limited portion of this end of the beach was available for bathing, and often, when he wasn't too sleepy, Abdul stirred things up too much for comfort. Still, the practice of the snipers was not particularly good, and Mac felt comfortably secure as long as he didn't venture out too far. It was their habit to wash what clothes they were wearing, and to bake in the sun while they dried. And so, bathing and splashing, sunning and smoking, sleeping and talking, a morning on the beach passed pleasantly enough.

Sometimes the pair wandered off to see a cobber in another part of the lines, exchange experiences and rumours with him, partake of his rations and water, and wander homeward through miles of dusty saps, not forgetting on their way to replenish their water-bottles at the landing and to acquire there any provisions which might, or might not look as if they lacked an owner, or, at any rate, the supervision of a policeman's eye.

Mails were now arriving occasionally, and never were letters more warmly welcomed. There would be a buzz of excitement while a mail-bag was being sorted, and then a strange quiet would hang over the terraces while ever one in his dug-outs eagerly explored his pages.

CHAPTER 18

Summer Drags On

The Anzac troops were now entering on that long, wearisome summer wait, without action, or even prospect of it, to relieve the monotony, until such time as strong reinforcements would enable them to make a push for the Narrows. The days grew hotter and the flies thicker, and disease began to make itself felt to an undesirable extent. The same old shelling and the same old rifle-fire went on week after week, varied only by the constant flutterings at Quinn's, where sometimes Turk, sometimes Anzac, got the better of the nightly bickerings. Rumours of victories at Cape Helles came frequently, but confirmation seldom followed. The fall of Achi Baba took place almost as often as the assassination of Enver Pasha. And still the Turks remained unmoved on the slopes of Sari Bair, and though the men of Anzac had the upper hand in sniping and morale there was not much prospect of getting the enemy rooted out of those confoundedly fine trenches of his for some time to come.

But these things did not greatly depress the fine fellows who clung so tenaciously to that square mile of crags and cliffs. The great spirit of cheery optimism, the light-hearted, careless good fellowship, and the muscle and grit of the invaders looked lightly at all this. Regiments might dwindle sadly from dysentery and shrapnel, the water-supply might be short and brackish, the flies might be getting more persistent; but reinforcements would come someday soon, the British at Cape Helles would get Achi Baba, and soon all would be well.

And so, with hard work, dysentery and flies, shelling, sniping and bombing, cheery philosophy, and castles in the air, sweat, heat and dirt, the summer days passed slowly by.

After a fortnight's absence from the front line, officially termed "resting," but which was spent, as has been described, in outpost fighting, sapping, road-making and all manner of hard work, the regiment returned to Russell's Top. As his squadron was relegated to a very comfortable section of the line, where disquieting bombs, shells and what-not, seldom disturbed him, and where, at times, one could stretch at full length and sleep, Mac infinitely preferred these conditions of life to those of the previous fortnight.

So, two weeks here passed placidly enough. When he was in the front line he smoked, read, wrote, and played cards, or, when particularly bored, rose up with his rifle and potted at elusive periscopes, swinging shovels, loop-holes or indiscreet Turks, of whom there were very, very few, in the Turkish lines. As often as not his little game would be cut short by the reply of one of their snipers.

Then the tangled mass of trench and ravine over which his position looked, Quinn's, Courtenay's, Dead Man's Ridge, and so on, was always an interesting study. They were for ever scrapping there, and at nights never for a moment rested. This was the weakest point in the Anzac lines, and both sides knew it; but lately persistent hard work, many lives and a great deal of courage were giving the Anzac fellows the upper hand. Beyond these trenches lay the wide valley bounded on the farther side by the frowning escarpments of Kilid Bahr Plateau—strongly entrenched heights which Mac rather hoped it would be some other person's job to storm when the necessity arose.

Across the valley and up a steep zigzag path climbing the almost overhanging farther side, he saw long trains of camels pass, and occasionally odd horsemen. Sometimes machine-gun fire at extreme range disturbed their placid way, but usually the gunners kept their ammunition for better purposes.

Their fortnight expired, the regiment, relieved by the light horse, returned to its previous bivouacs in the hot and stuffy ravine, where, in sections of four, they settled down to a domestic life, for the comfort of which they brought into bearing all their ingenuity, the possibilities of the Indians' larder and mule-feed, the lack of alertness on the part of the policemen at the depot, and the usual stock of knowledge acquired in the bush of how to look after oneself.

The bivouac of Mac's section consisted of a platform nearly seven feet square cut out of a steep clay ridge. So, a clay bank formed the back wall, two clay walls reached about half-way to the awning on either side, and the front was open, except in the afternoons when an oil-sheet was hung there to keep out the fierce glare of the sun. The clay cliff dropped precipitously in front, and facing them in the opposite cliff were similar bivvies, with the inhabitants of whom Mac and his cobbers were in the way of exchanging friendly conversation at odd moments of the night or day.

Perched here on their ledge of clay, the four lived a supremely happy life when at home. Each took his turn at the cooking, the firewood-hunting, and the tidying-up. Each had his strong points, and was permitted to develop them. Bill was hot stuff on curry à la Anzac, whose foundation was the choicest bully, a little water, plenty of Indian curry powder purchased from the Indians in consideration of some mouldy army cigarettes, and a little of everything else, from bran to marmalade. He shone, too, with his Welsh rarebit and his biscuit pudding, so that not even Smoky with his "Stew Supreme à la Depôt" could hope to look at him. Friday outran all others in his enthusiasm for gathering firewood, a rare product of the land in those days, and no one dared, nor felt inclined, to compete with him.

Mac had no rival when it came to frying, and the preparation of the sweets fell to him on those few but glorious days when the section was issued with one fig, two dates or half a dozen currants. The possibilities of the larder were considerably spun out by barter with the Indians, who had plenty and to spare of good food, by the use of one's wits and by purchase at exorbitant prices of certain articles from sailors. Still, despite this high living, the troops grew perceptibly thinner.

All offensive on Gallipoli was at this time confined to the Cape Helles front, where the capture of Achi Baba was their immediate object. The role of the Anzac troops was merely to keep the enemy always on the alert and in fear of an offensive movement from Anzac, and to make small demonstrations during heavy attacks on the big hill of Achi Baba.

On these occasions Mac would watch eagerly through his glasses the bursting shells along its crests, and would seek indications of a British advance, but always in vain.

Much as the Anzac troops yearned for some activity to break the monotony, there was little prospect of success of any present push from there. The regiments were thin; the Turks held strong superior positions, and possessed more machine-guns than were to Mac's liking.

The enemy made several night attacks, which brought nothing but casualties and regrets to the attackers. On one of these occasions Mac's squadron was in reserve to the Light Horse on Russell's Top, and were doing their best to sleep on the narrow clay terraces perched along the cliffs behind it.

About nine o'clock, heavy, ominous thunder-clouds came rolling silently in from the west. Lightning played in fitful dashes. Then followed swirling wind gusts, which stirred up fantastic columns of whirling dust, roared down the ravines, and raised a surf which grated furiously on the shingle below. Thunder crashed and bellowed, and the whole weird fantasy of crag, cliff and cyclonic dust columns was terribly and wonderfully lit by the vivid and almost continual flashing of the lightning.

Not content with the inferno of nature, the enemy chose this mad moment to add his artillery to the cataclysm, and turned a merry whizz-bang battery on to the Top. For an hour the racket lasted, and then fell in gradual diminuendo; and Mac thought of sleep notwithstanding vermin, dust and shrapnel. It was not to be. A fatigue party was wanted immediately. A number were told off. Warmly and extensively apostrophising the originators of this nocturnal expedition, they gathered up their rifles, *bandoliers* and water-bottles and wandered protestingly off uphill.

Arrived in the front fire-trench, they were directed to set about roofing bomb-proof dug-outs, in place of another party which was too tired to continue. The new arrivals, who had been working hard for three nights in succession, were righteously indignant, and also considered themselves too tired to carry on. Only two or three enthusiasts showed any inclination to work, and these were speedily discouraged by a further increase of activity on the part of the enemy artillery. Seventy-five m. m. whizz-bangs shrieked low over the surface, or burst with shattering crashes which shook down avalanches of earth on the heads of the troopers as they sat, half-asleep, against the dug-out walls.

Then the machine-guns joined in the din, and rattled and roared in spiteful bursts, now rising into a furious storm, now lulling slightly. The bullets whipped and whizzed past, or plopped into the heaps of debris above. Now that there was sufficient military reason for laziness on his part, Mac, recognizing, of course, that he would have worked had it been at all possible, sank with an easy conscience into somnolence.

When he awoke it was broad daylight, and the tornado of his last sleepy moments of consciousness had diminished to the usual spasmodic rifle reports. He stood up, ruefully rubbed the spots where ammunition pouches had made dents in his person, stepped over his still sleeping cobbers and crawled through the rabbit-hole entrance into the fire-trench. There he blinked like a sleepy owl, more with surprise than anything else.

There were dead Turks all over the show, and in a sap, opposite, were dozens of them. This was a sap which had kept Mac occupied for many nights recently. It was a secret sap, or supposed to be so as far as the enemy was concerned; and had been constructed with every care and precaution to that end. Running parallel with the Turkish front firing-line, thirty yards away, it connected a corner of the Anzac firing-line with the edge of a cliff a couple of chains to the left, and thus cut off a big bend in its front line.

With much satisfaction a light horseman gave Mac particulars of the occurrence:

"My bloomin' oath, we got 'em fine. We sorter guessed from the blanky rough-house they were making they was up ter something and got ready to make 'em welcome. Then with a lot of their bloom- ing *Allahin'* and raising a hell of a howl generally, they come over like a blooming mob of sheep. A big bunch got into that secret sap there. Then we landed 'em a dirty one, and bombed their blanky souls to hell. They didn't half squeal. Not content with one dose, the silly blanks came on again, and we had a bloomin' encore. Well, old man, I suppose the poor devils'll have sorrowing *harems*. 'Spose my poor old mater'd drop on me if she knew I was rejoicin' over the fallen. Any- how it's what we're here for, and they oughter keep out of our way if they don't want to get dinged, eh, cobber?"

"Anyhow, good luck to the blighters when they reach their bloo- min' heaven," answered Mac. "It's about *kai*-time. I'm off for some brekker. *Kia Ora*, old man."

And, so saying, he awakened his sleeping cobbers, left them admir- ing the night's catch, and trundled off homewards. Passing down the track he stopped for a moment by a ledge, and gazed with respect and sadness at half a dozen fine stalwart forms of Light Horsemen, wrapped each in his grey blanket, who had taken the long trail in the night's encounter.

The regiment was getting tired of continually sapping without any excitement to break the monotony, other than the more or less frequent arrival of shells in their vicinity, and the attentions of snipers on the beach.

Moreover, the flies increased in their countless millions, the ground was getting very dirty, the stench in parts was almost unendurable, and practically everyone was more or less affected by stomach trouble. The troops grew daily thinner, until, had he not followed their increasing slimness, Mac could hardly have recognised some of his old friends. With dark olive skins, cadaverous faces and often a good growth of beard, they were a hard-looking lot.

CHAPTER 19
Mac Takes a Change

The behaviour of Mac's stomach was not all that it might have been, besides which rheumatism began to develop, so he contemplated a short spell on the island of Lemnos. It was a place truly to be desired. There the distant reverberation of the Cape Helles artillery could only just be heard, one might walk in the open and bathe without having to worry about snipers or shrapnel, and, moreover, there were ships with canteens and, perhaps, a good meal. So, one evening, ticketed and labelled, and with the combined financial assets of his section in his pocket, he waited for embarkation at the cove. Many others were there, about half wounded and the rest medical.

Night-time at the cove was always beautiful. The starry brightness above the blackness of the sea, the steep rising face of the hill, with the twinkling lights and flickering fires of the bivouacs, the throng of toilers among the great piles of stores, the mules and water-carts crunching along the gravel, the wounded waiting embarkation—Mac saw what might be called the throbbing heart of Anzac. It throbbed, for the most part, in darkness; but, here and there, caught in the half-light from lamps among tiered piles of boxes, he had odd glimpses of the splendid fellows as they went about their work; and he was thrilled by the grandeur and manhood of it all.

Hours passed. Then a musical call through a megaphone, "Walking-cases this way," woke them to attention. They were all embarked on a lighter, and were towed, first by a pinnace, and then by a minesweeper, out into the bay, until high above them, aglow with green, red and yellow lights, reared the steel sides of a hospital-ship. A steam crane swung each giddily upward, and deposited him on the clean white deck.

Mac didn't quite know where he was that night. He accepted a dose of medicine and some kind words from a medical officer, absorbed a cup of hot cocoa and a piece of bread and butter—almost forgotten luxuries and found himself at length in a comfortable bunk with white sheets. Very faintly from the heights across the water floated sounds of strife; and Mac, with a sigh of supreme satisfaction, turned over and went to sleep. When he woke in the morning, a white girl— a sister—was standing beside his bunk. He was shy—he felt so rough. It seemed ages since he had seen a woman.

At ten o'clock, the light cases for Lemnos transferred to a minesweeper, and thence to a fleet-sweeper. All the afternoon the vessel steamed across sunlit seas and in the evening entered Mudros Harbour, passing through the great fleet that lay there, transatlantic liners, men-o'-war ancient and modern, hospital-ships, transports and small craft of every description, to an anchorage on the east of the harbour. The patients were landed in launches, and made their way, in a long straggling line of decrepits, to the field hospitals.

Mac found a resting place in the 1st Australian Stationary Hospital, and passed a week there. He was relegated to a large marquee, the sides of which were always rolled up. In the centre stood two tables, one occupied by medicines and the other by the dishes and food of the establishment. Stretched on the ground was a large tarpaulin, whereon, with a blanket apiece, eighty or more *hors de combat* heroes had their abode. Everything was as good as could be had in Mudros; but in those days Mudros lacked almost everything that could be desired. The water-supply was bad; food, in the Australian hospital was ample, and, for fare under such conditions, excellent, but in other hospitals it lacked lamentably. Inhabitants of the latter envied greatly those who, by good fortune or intrigue, were lodged in the former.

In the daytime the sun blazed down with fierce heat upon the marquees, the slightest breath of wind stirred into clouds the many inches of fine dust which covered the ground, and flies of many breeds were there in their pernicious millions. Vermin stalked by night; and odd moments of the day might profitably be spent in reprisals on these bloodthirsty beasts. Those were the sorry points of the place; but there were also good.

Immediately alongside the hospital, though officially out of bounds, was the village of Mudros East, a quaint place where there was always some fun to be had. Low stone, tile-roofed houses, with narrow dusty alleys—where congregated squalid children, mangy dogs, poultry and evil smells—clustered round a low hill surmounted by a large maternal Greek church. This latter was tawdry in the extreme, with wonderful symbolic pictures, icons, candle grease and cheap furniture. Over all, presided a dumpy, cheery little priest, who, with a beaming smile, indicated his perpetual readiness to accept small donations. Still, it had its air of sanctity, and it was pleasant to see there, Greek women praying with deep fervour. Occasionally, too, Mac noted British and French soldiers upon their knees.

Near the landing-place stood a street of filthy, hastily erected, wooden shanties, where the ever-trading Greek offered garden produce, very, very doubtful eggs and more or less objectionable stuff of other descriptions. The medium of exchange was varied in the extreme, and ranged from British, French and Egyptian coins to tins of bully beef, army jam, badges and the like.

There were some fine men in the hospital and next to Mac lay Mick. He was a light horseman, and Mac made a cobber of him.

"Chest's me trouble—touch of t.b. the Doc says. I cough away some of these nights like a sheep with lung-worm. I feel all right myself; but ev'ry time I talks about getting a shift on like, ole Doc gets busy with his water-diviner—'breathe in breathe out'—and then he says, 'Say "Ah-h-h."' Then he thumps away wid his fingers. I reckon I'm about as chuberculer as a young gum-tree, but the ole Doc he just says 'Carry on for a while longer and then we'll see.'"

Mick looked as fit as a two-year-old. After his fine figure, the first feature Mac noticed was a large but unfinished tattoo of the Royal Arms across the aforementioned unsound chest. Tubercular or not, that chest spent most of its hours in the fresh air, along with most of the rest of Mick's body.

"How d'you come by that bit of landscape, Mick?"

"Oh!——!——!——!" murmured Mick feelingly. "Me ruddy chest's crook outside as well as in. That's a ruddy souvenir of a night in Cairo, that is. Got a bit inked I s'pose. Don't remember too much about it meself. All I knows was I wakes up in the mornin' with a head like a sandstorm, no *piastres* left, and me chest as sore as hell wid this pretty picture on it—me, a bloomin' Aussie born and bred with the 'b—— 'art gorn Care-o chuum' badge on me manly chest—them wee lads whose mummies didn't know they was out. I tell yer I wasn't sweet the rest er that day. Bill, me cobber, 'e comes an' tells me 'e was in Cairo wid me. I tells 'im 'e needn't tell me that. 'Anyhow, if yer was,' I says, 'wy didn't yer stop 'em brandin' me? Nice feller you are to call yerself me cobber?'

"'Oh,' he says, 'I did me best, but you wasn't havin' any. You threatens to hit me over the 'ead if I don't go stop shovin' me opinions in w'ere they wasn't wanted. 'Me skin's me skin,' you says, 'An' I'll do what I b—— well like with it!' Then I tries ter drag you off, an' we had a bloomin' scuffle outside the show, an' you pushes me down some steps. I wasn't none too good neither.'

"'Then we goes in again, an' you starts takin' off yer tunic. You tells the *Gyppie* to show you some styles; and between tryin' 'em on so ter speak, an' one thing and er nother, you gits all yer b—— clothes off. The *Gyppies* come to light with some booze—filth it was, I bet—an' we both has some, an' you pays 'em about twenty *piastres* fer it. Then you hooks this Manchester badge and says "*Quiis kitir.*" An' they was tryin' ter push some rude indecent ones on ter yer, an' wishin' ter save yer from the worst like I tells yer the Manchester one was beautiful. An' I says it was what ev'ry patriotic Aussie should wear. You starts skitin' about Australian loyalty and Australia will be there an' that sorter thing, an' then says "yer'll 'ave it."

"'They gets to work an' all goes well, and when they was just 'alf finished, the bloomin' picket comes along an' pushes us out. I tries to get yer dressed but you was thinkin' you knew more about it than I did, an' you wasn't far wrong. I dunno meself how we got home. Anyhow, cobber, we both had our pockets gone gently through, for me *feloose* is gone as well as yours. I didn't have much, but wot I had's now somebody else's.'

"'Yer a b—— fine cobber, you are,' I says, 'Not to have choked 'em off.'

"'You've got ter thank me, anyway, fer not letting 'em put somethin' on yer which yer wouldn't care to let the world or yer missis, when you have one, gaze at.'

"An' that's how this lovely work in red and blue decorates me manly chest. The Doc he always smiles and twinkles his eyes so merry like when he sounds me chest. I'm thinkin' of havin' it turned inter a risin' sun. Me troop thinks it is an 'ell of a good joke, an' I reckon it would be too if it was on someone else's chest. Them b—— Manchesters!"

Mac and Mick wandered abroad together occasionally to investigate the land—Mac more for the pleasure of getting away from the hot dusty camp, and Mick for the prospects of raising more tolerable refreshment than lukewarm rusty water from ships' tanks. They wandered to far villages where the stolid Greek peasant life was not in the least disturbed by the activity in the harbour nor the distant rumble of Gallipoli guns—except that eggs and vegetables brought wonderful money. These villages were out of bounds and they found them empty of troops except for a solitary mounted policeman in each who could be easily dodged in the narrow lanes and shady fig-trees.

At the end of the first week in the field hospital both Mac and Mick were transferred to a new camp about three miles inland. It was less afflicted with flies, but there was only sufficient water for drinking purposes and enough food for about half the three hundred patients. The only water for washing was to be had occasionally in the early morning hours at the bottom of a well about a third of a mile away.

About ten minutes of angling with a canvas bucket on the end of a rope brought Mac about two inches of very muddy water. But on their first day's ramble Mac and Mick discovered about two miles from the camp a fine pool of stagnant water. It lay in the bottom of a rocky gorge, a shallow basin at the foot of what was a small waterfall during the winter rains. It was swarming with insect life, but, unheeding such minor details, Mac and Mick soon stripped off their clothes and made the best of it. Next day they came armed with towels, soap and all the permanganate of potash their kits could muster. At the worst this browny-pink pool left them a good deal cleaner and cooler than before, and the two troopers usually came that way once or twice daily.

They slept, too, on the open hillside some distance from the camp, as it was cooler, cleaner and quieter, and they put in only an occasional appearance for medicine and a meal. The staff of the camp seemed concerned with greater things than the presence or otherwise of a couple of troopers, and Mac and Mick saw no particular obstacle to their remaining a month or two. Mac had exhausted most of his and the section's finance in excellent fashion. The harbour was out of bounds, but in several surreptitious excursions out on to the harbour, with Mick and one or two others, he had succeeded in getting from ships' canteens and stores as big a stock of provisions as he could carry with him on his return journey to Anzac.

On two men-o'-war they had been splendidly received by the crews, who, fully appreciating the rottenness of life ashore, did all in their power to make pleasant the few hours' stay of such odd soldiers as found their way on board. The bluejackets crowded round the visitors, all anxious to be their hosts. They took Mac and Mick to a bathroom, and, while they had a good splash round, prepared a really attractive meal with extra delicacies bought at the canteen. The wanderers would make the most of it too.

Then, after an hour or so's yarn on the cool, clean awninged deck, they would take a regretful departure, and would go over the ship's side laden with good things from the sailors, the latest newspapers from home, smokable tobacco, and good canteen stores. They were fine men, the sailors whom Mac came across at Gallipoli, generous, hospitable fellows when they had the chance, and ready always to back up their comrades ashore, and to share with them the dangers, discomfort and disease of life ashore whenever they were called upon.

Thus, at the end of a fortnight on Lemnos, Mac had collected in the care of a friend near the landing-place as much as he could carry back. Mick, too, had followed his example and had collected a case of provisions for his cobbers up at Anzac. Mick, moreover, was heartily fed up, he said, of hanging about this mouldy island, and he knew that he could bluff the M.O. at the new camp that he had had dysentery and was now all right; and that, if there happened to be any official papers in the camp, no one would trouble to find them, nor probably could, if they wanted to. Mac was not so keen to hurry back, but the fortnight's rest from the line and better food had set him to rights, and he fell in eventually with Mick's suggestion. They approached an old M.O., who pushed them through without ever getting suspicious about Mick, and two hours later in the early afternoon they were bumping over the open country in a Ford ambulance towards the landing-place.

The late afternoon was spent in the *Aragon*, down in the depths of a well-deck, waiting for the fleet-sweeper to take them to Anzac. Mick was furious because he was not allowed to buy stuff at the ship's canteen, as it was reserved for those non-fighting staff soldiers who lived in all the comfort and safety of this beautiful ship. Mick was loud and exceedingly pointed in his remarks. However, he and Mac succeeded in penetrating to the depths of the ship, where, with the few odd coins still in their possession, they managed to bribe the cook to let them have as much currant bread, buns and sausages as would fill up all the spare corners in their kit. They ate as much on the spot as they possibly could, and eventually went on board the sweeper very well loaded.

Six hours' steam across the warm night waters brought them again within earshot of the usual night musketry fire. At one in the morning they were once more ashore at the Cove, with its tireless throng of men, mules and limbers. Mac deposited his load in the bivouac of a friend, and then parted for ever with his good cobber Mick, his casual companion of a Lemnos fortnight, whose way lay in the opposite direction.

CHAPTER 20

Anzac Awakes

Mac set off for his regiment, which was holding the front trenches of Russell's Top. Knowing it was a hopeless business poking about trenches among sentries in the dark looking for his unit, he lay down at the base of the top, and slept there on the ground till daylight.

He found his squadron in the most uncomfortable of trenches, and not particularly enjoying itself. It was holding the portion of the top nearest the enemy, who were between twenty and thirty yards away and well within range of hand grenades. But two could play at the same game, and the Turks had a better supply of bombs.

Two halves of the squadron took in turn the holding of the front saps and the main line. The former were narrow, shallow twisting ditches between piles of loose earth and rotting bodies. Parts were covered in as bomb-proof shelters, and in places sloping shafts led steeply down to mine galleries before the enemy's front line. Between those two series of drab mounds of earth which marked the opposing lines, lay as terrible an acre as ever was. The hasty burying during the armistice three months ago had been inadequate, and the saps had cut through many of the hastily-scratched graves. Since then many men had fallen, to rot unburied in the sun and to be again and again torn by shells and bombs and bullets.

A few shattered sticks were the forlorn remnants of the luxurious scrub. Wire twined in untidy coils here and there, but there was nothing to hide the blackened bodies. Sometimes at night low fires licked among the corpses, apparently started by the Turks by throwing over their parapet paraffin or petrol, and there would be spasmodic explosions for an hour or more of the ammunition in the equipment round the dead forms, sounding like the burning of a Guy Fawkes effigy.

Mac had never more than swiftly surveyed the scene direct—for there was a deadly accuracy in the practice of the snipers at twenty yards range—but viewed its details and the Turkish parapets through a periscope. These, too, the snipers shattered with annoying frequency, though the Turks themselves had no rest whatever in the matter of being sniped at. And in these wretched saps amid a horror of desolation Mac and his cobbers passed every second twenty-four hours.

In the daytime the sun beat into them with unrelieved violence, and many troopers squeezed into the bomb-proof shelters and tunnel entrances to seek shade. There was nowhere to cook food, and bully beef, biscuits and water formed the fare. But they had small appetite for anything, as the stench of the dead and the flies which swarmed left few men hungry. At one corner hung a blanket. Sometime a sapper in his work had come to a body, and had turned the sap to the right to avoid it, and the blanket had been tacked up as a screen to the body in the recess.

One hard case found this recess a shady spot and with more room for his cramped legs, and declared that it was no worse alongside the several months old corpse than anywhere else in the saps. In one place the lower leg and boot of a dead Turk stuck out from the corner of a trench, and at another a bony hand protruded. Grim humourists shook it as they passed.

The warm nights dragged drowsily by. In these trenches the troops were not supposed to sleep because of the bombs thrown so frequently by the Turks. If one were awake, they could be easily dodged, but, if a bomb caught a man asleep, there was little chance of escape. Every second twenty-four hours were passed in the main firing line, a few yards farther back than the saps, or close up in reserve.

Sometimes, during these second days, it was possible to get a bathe when on a journey for rations or water, and a little cooking could be attempted on a ledge in the side of a communication trench. But altogether everything was most uncomfortable, and with the cramped life Mac's rheumatism was returning. There was little sleep too, rarely exceeding two hours a day as the fortnight passed. Strong enemy reinforcements had been reported by aerial reconnaissance within easy march of Anzac, and an attack was expected any night. The Regiments were very much under strength from disease, and the burden of watching fell heavily on the remaining men. Mac was disappointed too that, in their present limited quarters, they could make no use of the provisions he had brought from Lemnos.

Relief came at last, without the enemy having made an attack, and the Mounted Rifles again handed Russell's Top over to the Australian Light Horse. They thankfully trundled away down the hill with all their gear to a pleasant bivouac near the sea, and proceeded without delay to make themselves as clean and as comfortable as could be. Mac went off for the provisions, and soon the section had a small awninged dug-out in excellent domestic order. Here, terminated by a stone wall, the main Anzac left flank met the sea.

The trench line here was but thinly held, as it did not directly oppose Turkish trenches. Beyond it, at the seaward end of the sharp ridges which ran up to the main broken mass of Sari Bair, Chanak Bair and Battleship Hill, were No. 1 and No. 2 Outposts, faced by the formidable Turkish outposts on the forbidding crags above. So, separated by some distance from the enemy, the regiment proceeded to enjoy itself.

It was the pleasantest possie Mac had ever found it his privilege to occupy. The bivvies were roomy and comfortable, the ground was comparatively clean, and was sufficiently gradual in its rise to prevent constant avalanches of earth from above. The sea lay at their door, and the freshwater tanks were near enough to make certain a regular water supply. Mac and his mates made merry with the provisions he had secured at Lemnos, and the products of their culinary art knew no bounds, either in variety or perfection. With an abundance of firewood and water, with the sea always near to be bathed in, awninged bivvies and a well-stocked larder, they lived in undreamed-of luxury. They had hoped for the usual fortnight there; but it was not to be.

As the long, hot, dusty July days came to a close, the pulse of Anzac seemed to quicken. Men went about their work with increased energy, the cove was busier than ever, and life altogether in that sunscorched, sordid spot seemed less burdensome. Staff officers walked about with unaccustomed briskness, and made unnaturally long visits to observation points, gazing absorbedly at Turkish terrain. Visible signs there were that the dormant days of Anzac were drawing to an end, and that at last the summer lethargy would give place to times of action. Rumours filled the air. Wild they were, but there was definite evidence that something was in the wind, and everybody rejoiced accordingly. There would be a real ding-dong go; and then, probably, Constantinople.

It was now obvious that the scheme of operations involved a flank attack to the north, which, it seemed, from the extensive preparations, might be the main thrust. Anzac positions were faced immediately by the frowning outposts of Destroyer Ridge, Table Top, Old No. 3, Rhododendron and Baeuchop's (Beauchop's?) Ridge, beyond which stretched that maze of broken ridges, which rose sharply to the main peaks of Sari Bair, Chanak Bair and Kojatemen Tepe, which commanded the whole width of the Peninsula and the Turkish positions and lines of communication. Gain them, and Gallipoli would be won.

On the dark, moonless nights of the 3rd, 4th and 5th of August transports stole silently to anchor off the cove, and many battalions of Kitchener's Army and batteries of Field Artillery came ashore. When the sun again lifted above the eastern hills, the anchorage was deserted and the new arrivals hidden from aerial observation beneath prepared covering. Anzac grew tense in anticipation of a battle royal.

For the five days spent in this bivouac—the days of the awakening of Anzac—to Mac and a dozen of his mates fell the duty of guarding the exit from the main position to the outposts. The exit consisted of a large barbed-wire gate across a great communication trench, close to the stone wall on the beach. They did four-hour watches there night and day, taking a tally of all who came and went, and watching keenly for spies. During their daylight hours of duty, Mac and Bill sat on sandbags under the shady wall of the sap. Their bayoneted rifles leaned against the bank close at hand, while they, scantily clad in the scorching hours, lazily noted in tattered note-books the particulars of sweating, dust-covered wayfarers.

When they were not busy, they sat there automatically flicking away the flies, and watching through a gap in the trench the horde of naked men on the beach. Passing mules often left Mac and Bill grousing in a cloud of dust. Aussies, Maoris and New Zealanders stopped now and then for a few minutes' rest beneath their awning. They would yarn for a while, and the guards would accept from their freshly-filled cans a drink of cool spring water. When the relieving guard came, Mac and Bill just stripped off their shorts, and ran across the stones for a splash in the sea.

At night they were more alert on guard. Sleepy as Anzac appeared in the hot sunlight, dark hours shrouded a scene of energy and purpose. As soon as the evening light had gone, long strings of heavily-laden mules, with tall Indian muleteers struggling among them, came along the sap and passed out through the gate. There were pauses, but soon more mule trains followed, and the earlier ones passed back empty for further loads. All the time the guard watched carefully lest there should be strangers attempting to pass through hidden among the mules. Great piles of bully beef, biscuits, sealed paraffin tins of water and ammunition grew steadily bigger in hidden spots behind the outposts, and the troops were light-hearted accordingly.

Platforms had been cut in hill-sides for the accommodation of troops away from enemy observation, communication trenches had been widened, some had been bridged and others had been created silently and swiftly in a single night. Without orders from officers, the troops energetically overhauled rifles, ammunition and gear; and private possessions were looked into, diaries written and letters despatched. Between the opposing lines warfare continued its accustomed way, and the normal exchange of bombs, shells and bullets went on, though Turkish artillery fire was increasing in strength.

On Thursday, August 5th, the regiment sorrowfully packed up all unnecessaries and piled them in the regimental dump. Mac grieved to part with the unfinished half of the Lemnos provisions, for heaven only knew when they might see them again, and probably someone else would thrive on them.

That night the regiment moved out through the wire gate, and crowded on the platforms at the back of No. 1 Outpost, there to remain till the following evening, when the battle was to open.

CHAPTER 21

No. 3, Table Top and Suvla Bay

The regiment, stretched in close lines on the terraces, slept soundly. For many days ahead there would be little opportunity of resting, and for many there would be but one more sleep. They did not rouse till well after dawn, for there was nothing to do that day but fill in time. Mac again overhauled all his equipment, paying particular attention to his rifle, bayonet and ammunition, seeing that everything was accessible and that all ran smoothly. Then the section rigged a blanket between piled arms, and sat down in its shade for a game of cards. That palled after a time, and Mac drew from his knapsack a book, *The Cloister and the Hearth*, and was soon deep in its pages. Then came lunch, and in the afternoon, orders were read, with inspiring messages from the generals, and a few words from the C.O.

A few aeroplanes burred overhead, the exchange of firing followed its normal daily course, quieting rather in the heat of midday; but to the waiting troops the long hours dragged. That wonder of what the future held, that ominous quiet before the storm, the preparations for battle—all made the day long.

At last the sun sank behind the rugged islands in a glorious riot of colour, the high eastern hill-tops which should be British by dawn gradually grew black against the appearing stars. The regiment, water-bottles filled and in final trim, stood leaning on their rifles. Occasionally someone gave a hitch to his gear, others talked in subdued tones, or gazed solemnly out to sea where the black outlines of Imbros and Samothrace stood against the last glow of departing day.

At this glorious hour there drifted up from the darkness in the ravine below such a sound as went deep to Mac's heart. Rich in tone, perfect in key, unmarred by a single jarring note, and to the accompaniment of battle sounds above, came the music of the soul, and Mac was awed. It was the chanting of five hundred Maoris and their prayer before this, their first great trial in modern warfare. Upon the next few hours depended the reputation of their race. Would they be worthy of the glorious traditions of their old chiefs?

Then came the word to move, and the regiment, in single line, filed down the slope and into the main sap to the north. It was already full of troops filing to the attack, but, after many halts and side-trackings, they reached the exit which led to the ravine. Here, at the parting of the ways, stood the fine old *padre*, and, with a "God bless you, my boy," he shook each by the hand as they passed out to battle.

The several troops of Mac's squadron divided for their various objectives. To his section fell the duty of going up the ravine to cut enemy communication trenches, leading across it to their strong outpost on the ridge above on the left. Magazines were empty, and the orders were that the night's work must be done with the bayonet. The forty silent figures crept up the sharp stony bottom for a short distance, and then halted to await the critical moment of the attack. Then, while they waited, the long white beam from a man-o'-war at sea settled along the ridge on the left and showed the strong wired entrenchments of the outpost. *Whir-r-r* went a shell overhead, and the first shot of the battle burst in an eruption of black smoke among the Turkish wire.

More followed in rapid succession; but the first shot had been the signal for the troop in the defile below to set off at a jog-trot up its murky, twisty depths. They trotted along for five minutes, machine-gun bullets from high above sometimes hitting up small spurts of sand as they doubled round corners. Then, as they suddenly rounded a sharp ridge, a dozen or so rifles burst on them from fifteen paces distant. Some men went down in front of Mac, a cloud of dust sprang up and he stumbled over one of the prone forms.

Instantly they were in among them, the terrified Turks shrieked, a few odd shots rang out, Mac killed two with his revolver, and then, with bloody bayonets, shadowy figures emerged from the murky depths of the trench, and passed on to explore the ground beyond. They pushed up through the thick scrub to beneath the outpost where a battle now raged, for the purpose of catching fugitives and preventing reinforcements. But none came, and the troop sat quietly in the scrub awaiting developments. The sound of musketry echoed beautifully across the ravines in the clear stillness of the night.

The Turks were lighting fires in the stunted pine growth a short distance ahead, which lit with a red flickering light the overhanging clay cliffs of Table Top rising sharply at the farther side of the defile. Then the cold white glare of a searchlight settled on its flat top, and in a few minutes, heavy howitzer, 18-pounder and naval shells, shrieked overhead and burst, flashing and roaring, on the crest. The overhanging crag, her summit rent by an inferno of shell fire, her inaccessible escarpment lit by the lurid glow of scrub fires, and the fantastic smoke clouds eerily revealed by the searchlight, made altogether a wild night battle scene of weird glory.

The bombardment ceased suddenly, the searchlight switched off, and part of the regiment, who had crawled through the scrub on the more accessible flank during the shelling, successfully rushed the Top. Mac and his mates returned to their first scene of action and continued to guard the communication sap. One or two Turks, who had hidden in the scrub during the *mêlée*, gave their presence away, yelled with terror and fell dead at the first shot. Poor old Joe, who had been severely wounded by the first fusillade, lay dying, and soon his moans ceased altogether. Others were dead, and some wounded.

About three in the morning they went on again to join the rest of the regiment on Table Top. Struggling up the trench-like bottom of the ravine, through the inky blackness of the thick scrub, they found themselves at length in a *cul-de-sac*, with clay cliffs on either side. The officer went on to reconnoitre, and then, to the great discomfiture of the forty fellows huddled together in the clay watercourse, a hundred or so Turks put in an appearance on the brink of the steep cliff on the left. Babbling excitedly, they looked curiously down on the silent crouching troopers. Trapped, and entirely at the Turks' mercy, Mac momentarily expected annihilation, and wondered vaguely why it did not come. Retreat was hopeless, and he counselled scrambling up the steep bank and attacking them.

A tense half hour passed. Then came a guarded whistle from high up on the right, and he heard the faint command from his officer, "Climb up to the right." Quitting the troop, he scrambled up the soft yielding cliff, slid back to the starting point several times, still puzzled why the Turks on the opposite brink did not shoot, and at last found his officer near the top, quite bewildered as to the whereabouts of his men. Mac, exhausted with his exertions, was sent to report the night's events to the colonel, while his officer returned to guide the others up.

Table Top was a level, scrub-covered plateau, about four chains across, flanked on the north, west and south by steep cliffs, and on the east gently sloping up towards the higher hills. Mac found the colonel on the far side, answered his questions, heard from him that progress everywhere had been splendid and that the brigade had disposed of all its objectives, and then found a few spare moments to view the country from this high point.

Dawn was breaking—just the same old beautiful dawn they had so often watched silhouetting the trenches opposite and the hills beyond, but now, with the exhilaration of victory thrilling through his body, Mac stood there with the most glorious dawn of all his days, or of anyone else's he thought, lighting the eastern sky.

From the heights of the Table Top, Mac surveyed the scene below him. To his right as he faced the north, the Table Top was connected by a series of ridges with the hill summits about a mile away, which the sun was just topping. To his front the ground fell abruptly in a deep ravine, beyond which lay ridge after ridge, and beyond again the high range behind Anafarta, three miles away, all standing out clearly in sun-topped ridges and shadow, in the refreshing air of early morning. Out to sea were the two islands, rugged and beautiful as ever, which, together with the whole glory of the morning, the hills and the sea, were unconscious and unaffected by the battle of men developing on those beaches and hills to decide the fate of nations.

The Anzac shore swept away to the north-west in a splendid curve to Lala Baba, the point of Suvla Bay; and there, where no vessel floated at sundown, lay now the strategy of the battle, a great fleet of transports, warships, lighters, pinnaces and destroyers, encircled already by a great torpedo-net. Farther out, every detail reflected in the clear blue water, lay a dozen clean, sweet hospital ships. Already round the little mound of Lala Baba were gathered small bodies of men, horses and artillery, and occasionally Turkish shrapnel burst above them. The warships were sending shells up the Anafarta valley and on to the Turkish positions behind the great white patch of the Salt Lake.

Having thoroughly taken in the situation, Mac turned again to business. Some of the fellows were digging trenches on the enemy side of the plateau, the medicals were bandaging the wounded, Turkish and New Zealand, in a sheltered spot in the scrub, and Mac was told off to disarm and guard several hundred prisoners who were trooping up the steep slope from the rear. This was the garrison of the old No. 3 Outpost who had found their retreat cut off by the capture of Table Top, and were the same Turks who had, earlier in the morning, gazed down on Mac as he had crouched in the ravine bottom fifteen feet below them. He decided that they must have been demoralized then, or else he and his comrades had been no more.

The prisoners threw down their arms and *bandoliers* in a pile, and seemed to feel no regret. They beamed with happiness, offered cigarettes, biscuits, money and mementoes to their guards, and embarrassed them by crowding round in an effort to shake their hands. Eventually they were despatched under escort to the beach, and Mac seized a few spare moments to watch an attack, half a mile to the south, which was being made by Light Horsemen from the main position on Russell's Top.

Destroyers close in below sent high explosive shell whirring upwards to burst in a pall of black smoke and dust on the narrow neck between the Turkish and Australian lines. There was a tornado of machine-gun fire which reached Mac's ears only as a high-pitched continuous note. The shelling lasted about ten minutes only, a hopelessly inadequate preparation, he knew, on such positions. The storm of machine-guns rose to terrific violence, ripping and roaring. A grey fog of smoke and dust partially screened the scarred hill-tops, and shielded the *mêlée* from his vision, but, knowing those tiers of Turkish trenches as he did, he was awed with the thought of what must be passing.

For fifteen minutes it lasted in all its fury, then lulled slightly, to burst forth again for a few minutes only to diminish once more to a steady burr, which left nothing decided in his mind. What had happened he did not know, but when he turned his attention there later in the morning he gathered, from the fact that the machine-guns still rattled in the same locality as before, that ground had not been gained.

His squadron were instructed to make perches in the seaward cliff of the crag where they would be safe from shrapnel which was now bursting occasionally in the vicinity. Mac endeavoured to do so, but so steep was the cliff that he only managed to make a ledge sufficiently wide to sit on, while his legs dangled over the abyss below, and the sun blazed on him in undiluted fury. But the greatest discomfort was the steady fall of a stream of powdered clay from the constructors of perches and paths higher up.

A veranda of Turkish bayonets with Turkish rifles roofed crossways on them, failed to improve the situation greatly, so he gave it up as a bad job, and moved to the shade of a fine arbutus bush on the less steep enemy side of the top. He preferred shade, comfort, and clean arms and ammunition, with the risk of Turkish shrapnel, of which he had no great fear, to the drawbacks of the cliff face without the risk.

The squadron lay in reserve all day, and Mac, from his shady altitude, revelled in being just so situated with a great battle in progress, with almost the whole battlefield in view, and him with nothing more to do than sit there in comfort watching it. He surveyed it all through his glasses, tracing the present limits of the advance. The high hills seemed still to be Turkish, for different bodies of white-patched troops made a rough line some distance below the summit, running down laterally towards Suvla Bay. Distant ridges lined by the same white-patched men showed that all the foothills had been taken; but Mac watched eagerly, though in vain, for the appearance of British troops on the higher ridges. Chocolate Hill and Osman Oblu Tepe at the inner end of the Salt Lake, which were the main obstruction to the success of what seemed to be the plan of attack. He saw only a few Turks on these hills, and odd ones scurrying about near Anafarta, but never a body of them, large or small.

There was a great mass of troops gathered round the small mound of Lala Baba, on whose top was now a wireless station and a signal mast. There were horses, artillery, limbers, mobs of men and increasing piles of stores. From huge four-masted transatlantic liners came lines of seven or eight crowded boats in tow of a pinnace, and already the same lines were threading their way back to the hospital ships farther out. But the troops on shore were scarcely moving. During the whole day, only a few small bodies advanced a short distance, with little opposition it seemed, at any time. Why did they not make a general advance?

Shells fell occasionally on different sections of the general line, the diminishing music of the machine-guns floated, almost unnoticed, across the hot stillness of the midday hours, the freshness of the morning had given way to the summer glare, softened rather by the blue haze from fires which here and there crept through the scrub. Men-o'-war, close inshore, were shrouded in a murky pall from their flashing broadsides, while their shells tore holes in the village of Anafarta, or sent scrub and earth flying as they searched enemy ridges or passed to unseen billets beyond the summits.

Hospital ships weighed anchor and passed into distance, and destroyers patrolled unceasingly to guard against submarine attack.

Up the narrow, twisting sultry bottoms of ravines swarmed confused trails of sweating men and animals, mules laden with ammunition and water, with their Punjab muleteers, Sikhs with their mountain pieces, and fresh troops, British and Purkha, New Zealand, Australian, passing up to the line. Trickling rearwards, moving when opportunities offered, went limping the bandaged wounded, the stretcher-cases, bloodstained and grey, but patient, splendidly patient, the unladen mules, often waiting long periods for a clear passage, and all the odd men, messengers, prisoner escorts and others who move up and down the communications during a battle.

A few fellows of the regiment were caught by snipers hidden still in the scrub behind the advancing line. Otherwise the Table Top was undisturbed, and the trenches grew deeper. Some went back to bury those who had fallen in the night encounters. Mac, Bill and Charley stuck to their shady spot most of the day. In a hollow at their feet half a dozen dead Turks turned black in the sun. Midday came, and they consumed the last of the Mudros luxuries; then they cleaned their gear, slept awhile and awoke at five, expectant of great activity after the lethargy of the day.

The Suvla Bay force had at last roused itself, and now steady extended lines of men were advancing across the dazzling whiteness of the Salt Lake towards Chocolate Hill and Osman. White puffs of bursting shrapnel broke here and there above them; but only occasional men fell. Naval artillery raked the hills in front of them, where no Turk could be seen. The lines went forward slowly, too slowly, for there seemed to be little opposition to the advance and no hand-to-hand fighting. They did not even appear to have reached the base of Chocolate Hill when deepening shadows made it no longer possible to follow their progress.

CHAPTER 22
The Night Battle on Chanak Bair

Of the general progress of the battle through the night and indeed until he was wounded, Mac knew little. He heard but vaguely what was going on on other portions of the front and could see little, and gathered only indefinite impressions of happenings elsewhere.

He passed the second night of the battle in alternately trenching and resting, when he occasionally had a few moments of sleep. It was very dark, warm and clear with a glorious showing of stars. The noise of battle increased and seemed to fill the whole sky and earth as it had not in the daytime. Star rockets shot skyward from the enemy lines and burst into dazzling falling lights while the fellows crouched low in the scrub to escape notice. The flash of the artillery and of the bursting shells were here, there and everywhere, but mostly along the ridge tops, and the musketry roared spasmodically in squalls along the ridges, or drifted down from the high summits.

At length the stars slowly faded before the eastern glow, and the hill-tops stood out darker than before. Did dawn find them gained? Mac waited eagerly for more light; but, when it came, found little to discover. The summits seemed to be won, but he could find no trace of the British nearer Anafarta.

Sunday passed much in the same way as Saturday. The Suvla Bay force was still hanging about the landing-place, and there was no indication of a heavy engagement on their front. The New Zealanders had reached the high ridges of Chanak Bair, but no one knew, if they had progressed at all, how far they had gone over on the Dardanelles side. Nearly all the hospital ships had vanished with full cargoes of wounded; but otherwise the whole scene was little different from that of the previous day. The hot hours passed slowly, the battle roared on, and Mac and his mates wondered what might be their next move, for they were not at present opposed to any direct enemy force.

In the middle of the afternoon they received orders to prepare to move, with the exception of one squadron which was to garrison the positions. They moved off almost immediately, passing down the steep northern slope of the plateau and forcing their way through the dense thicket until they reached the bottom of the hollow. They turned to the right and jostled their way up through the struggling traffic along the narrow, suffocating bed of the ravine. There were places where many fine fellows had been laid low by snipers, places where they hurried, if possible. There were times when they were jammed between mules and the banks, and others when they had to wait many minutes for opportunities of pushing on. After an hour of this sort of thing, they came practically to the head of the ravine, and pushed into the scrub on one side to make temporary bivouacs.

Here all slacked and rested their weary bodies, stretched out full length under the stunted bushes. Weak, most of them, with dysentery when the battle started, they had now had two days of it, and with the heat, the short commons of water, and little sleep, they felt a wee bit tired, and they made the most of the short hours.

The cool of evening came again, and with it orders to prepare for further movements, this time to the firing line in support of their own men on the summit of the hills above. They made the best possible meal from the dry rations, dry enough when there was unlimited water, but quite impossible to more than nibble in these almost waterless days. Mac did not feel very hungry; but he had room inside his thin frame for a tankful of water. He had started on Friday evening with a liberally rum-tinctured bottleful, which had since been restocked with water as strongly tainted with petrol. For the purpose of the advance, sealed petrol tins of water had been brought from Alexandria, but the fillers of the tins seemed to have paid no particular attention as to whether they had first been emptied of petrol. His bottle was almost half-empty, and he did not care for the prospect of going up to those struggling lines without a fresh supply; but, just in time, a mule train came up with full *fantassas*, and he got a half-bottle.

When dusk had almost deepened to darkness, they joined the surging traffic of mules, men and stretchers on the dusty track, and filed laboriously up the steep hill. The din of battle heightened with the deepening night. Indian mountain batteries barked furiously behind them, and the heavier artillery sent shells shrieking up from far below, to burst somewhere up there where the crest stood silhouetted against the stars. From above came the incessant roar of bursting bombs and shells and rattle of musketry.

At dawn the summit had been gained, but just how good or bad our position was Mac had not the vaguest idea. He had not heard of, nor had he seen any progress, except the taking of this summit, since Saturday morning, and had no idea as to whether the battle was progressing favourably or otherwise. What was expected of them up there tonight none knew. Each carried a pick or a shovel and two bombs.

They passed the dressing-stations, perched on either side on the steep slope, where hundreds of wounded lay, then over a ridge where the track stopped and out into the pitch black open. The bullets zipped past or thudded into the ground. The troop lay down while they got their bearings. A fellow close by Mac gave a yell and was dead. A few wounded men, limping or crawling back, passed them. Then in extended order they went forward again, guided by a telephone wire, keeping touch with difficulty in the scrub and the darkness.

Frequently there would come from the blackness in front of their feet a warning "Keep clear o' me, cobber, I'm wounded," or groans and the gleam of a white bandage, and sometimes they stumbled over prone still forms. Slowly they picked their way forward, making towards the centre of the firing, which was in a semicircle round them, and the whistling bullets came from both sides as well as from in front, and the din grew fiercer. They reached at length a hollow full of wounded, then went slowly up a slope littered with equipment and dead, and, at last, topping the rise, they came upon a scene so weird and infernal that Mac instantly stopped and stared with awe.

Lit fantastically by flickering flames which were licking slowly through the scrub was a small ghastly, battle-rent piece of ground, not one hundred yards in width and rising slightly. Beyond and close on either side, it was bounded by the starry heavens, and seemed a strange, detached dreamland where men had gone mad. The Turks lined the far edge, their ghostly faces appearing and vanishing in the eerie light, as they poured a point-blank fusillade at the shattered series of shallow holes where the remnants of the New Zealanders were fighting gallantly.

Sweeping round to the left was the flashing semicircle of the enemy line, bombs exploded with a lurid glare, their murky pall drifting slowly back towards Mac. Shells came whirring up from the black depths behind, and burst beyond the further lip. Above the rending of the bombs, the rattle and burr of the rifles and machine-guns and the crash of shells, sometimes sounded faintly men's voices—the weird "*Allah, Allah, Allah*" of the enemy in a chanted cadence, and the fierce half-humorous taunts of the attackers.

Everywhere lay dead and dying men—mostly the former, Turkish and British. Equipment and rifles were strewn in the greatest confusion over the torn earth, and all the time the creeping flames cast weird lights upon the passing drama.

"Say, old boy," came a voice from his feet, "you'd better not stand there too long—it's pretty thick."

Mac leaned down to the wounded man, and found him one of the Aucklands. "It's been simply blanky hell up here all day and now I'm just waiting for them to give me a hand out. You boys have come up none too soon. Mind you give the devils hell!"

"You there with the pick," Mac found himself addressed, "get over to those holes up front there and dig in for all you're blanky well worth."

"Good luck, matey, *Kia Ora*," came the parting blessing from the wounded Aucklander in the scrub.

So, brimming over with good fellowship were the tones, so short, yet so deeply affectionate that Mac instinctively felt much more light-hearted as he stumbled across the shattered battlefield to the thin line of toiling, hard-pressed fighters, close to the rim where the cliff fell away on the Dardanelles side. He found a line of shallow holes, some a foot deep, some eighteen inches, aided a little by a few almost useless sandbags. The cliff brink was six or eight yards away, and under it lay the enemy—whose spectral figures, popping up and disappearing rapidly, blazed point blank into the exposed line.

A few yards on the left the Turks poured across from the cliff to a small knob which protruded into the attackers' line, and upon which they bore down constantly and bombed furiously. From the ravine below the enemy, came the constant "*Allah, Allah, Allah*," of many Turks encouraging themselves for the attack, and occasional yells when shells or bombs fell among them.

Mac knelt on the ground and endeavoured to deepen the hold by steady picking, while two other men kept a steady fire on the agile heads of the enemy. But try his best, he was now beginning to feel severely his decreasing strength and could make but little impression on the trench on this parched, sunbaked hill-top. Another trooper offered to take his place, and he went to the less arduous work of carrying such tattered sandbags as still contained earth from the second line about fifteen feet back and piling them up in some sort of a parapet for the front line. The second line was only half a dozen square holes whose fine garrisons lay dead within them, except a few who raved in delirium for water which was not to be had. They and their arms lay prostrate across each other, many half-buried by flying earth from shells and bombs.

He finished this work and then responded to an oft-repeated call from farther along, "Reinforcements for the right. Reinforcements for the right. Enemy getting round behind!" Here was a shallow bit of a hole with three or four men, the right flank of this part of the line, while the cliff edge was only four or five yards distant, and the enemy was thought to be crawling back and gathering for a heavy assault. Mac set about improving the trench and forming a small right angle to prevent enfilade and to protect the flank. The sap had been deeper earlier in the day, for the first foot he shovelled out consisted of a sticky muddy mass of blood, soil, ammunition and gear of all sorts. He sifted it carefully for good ammunition and bombs, and formed the rest into a parapet with the assistance of sandbags.

Sometimes when he was tired, he took a turn at keeping the enemy from becoming too venturesome on the cliff brink. Queer shapes stood out against the stars, but whether they were always Turks he could not tell, as from long sleeplessness and strain his sight was inclined to play him tricks. Anyhow he ran no risks. Somehow or other the troops farther on the left were constantly shouting warnings concerning figures passing back to the right, but these he could not see; while, curiously enough, he could plainly follow Turkish figures flitting across the sky-line on the left from the cliff to the small knob which could enfilade the trench from the left. His rifle jammed from heat and dust. He took two from dead men and kept them both on the parapet ready for instant action. The others did much the same sort of thing, helping each other, sticking grimly to the job and not worrying much, apparently, about their future.

The battle raged on through hour after hour with unabated fierceness; and the din of it all, the whirring and crashing of the shells, the furious rattle of musketry, the yells of men and the cries of the wounded, became almost an unnoticed monotone in Mac's ears. The Turks threw bombs steadily, but fortunately only in ones and twos. They were fairly slow to explode, and, if they landed on the parapet, the troops crouched in the bottom of the trench, or, if into the trench, they got out until the explosion and the fumes had cleared away.

The enemy was almost safe from bombing, for grenades which were thrown at him found no resting-place until far down into the ravine, where their explosion sounded only as a dull unsatisfactory thud. Sometimes big shells whirring up from the warships or the heavy land batteries burst short and caught some of the already too sparse attackers, or brought the sufferings of the wounded to an end. Mac's line lost men who went bleeding to the rear. Sometimes their places were taken—more often they were not.

He wondered vaguely what would happen, but all were too busy with affairs of immediate importance, and somehow it did not seem to matter in the least—the outlook was not bright. The Turkish mound on the left could enfilade the trench at short range when daylight came, the enemy was in great force in front and was creeping back to the rear—already a fire-swept zone impossible to cross. Where was that great force from Suvla Bay? They had landed three miles away at midnight on Friday and it was now just before dawn on Monday.

The night came in time near to its end. He could not describe it as having gone quickly, nor yet slowly—it had simply passed. Dawn brought no particular pleasure, only the transition from the unearthly phantasmagoria of bitter night fighting to the practical fierce hand-to-hand struggling of day. The paling sky figured the sky-line and the Turkish heads in definite silhouette, and many of the large shrubs of the night where Turks might lurk revealed themselves as small tufts of grass. Vigilance increased. If rifles did not sweep that crest continually the old Turk would leave his head and shoulders above the edge long enough to take aim, instead of blazing away rather at random.

It was now definitely seen that the Turks had got well round the right flank during the darkness, in spite of a machine-gun which had been said to sweep this zone; but of it Mac saw no sign. Some Turks were creeping through a hollow immediately to the right, and he being the tallest man at this point directed his attention at the wriggling backs with some success. One wounded Turk there signalled by waving his rifle to some of the advanced party, but was soon after lifted by a mate who ran with him to safety.

108

CHAPTER 23

Mac is Wounded

That August dawn revealed a ghastly scene on this Gallipoli hill-top, where the tired, outnumbered attackers fought desperately for the summit of the Peninsula, possession of which would mean victory and the command of the Straits. It seemed to Mac that decision must come soon, for this desperate, more or less continual hand-to-hand encounter could not last much longer. Bad as their position was, it could not be long now before those many thousands of Imperial troops would be taking the enemy in flank from the Suvla Bay direction, or at least would be strongly reinforcing them from the rear.

And now, even before it was full daylight, the activity along the line, though it had scarcely seemed possible, grew more violent, and Mac felt that each side tensely watched the other, expecting every moment a final, desperate coming to grips. The Turks appeared to be gathering in great numbers, and were even now on the point of making a whole-hearted attack.

But the British artillery intervened. The shelling had been increasing steadily, and at this moment several men-o'-war close inshore opened their broadsides and were joined by all the field artillery which could be brought to bear, and there broke along the crest such a tornado of bursting shells as had never been seen during the whole campaign.

The battleships were concealed by a thick pall of brown smoke through which spurted the flashes of their batteries, field guns of all sizes barked from ravines and ridges; the shells roared and shrieked up towards the summit, and burst in a continual shattering crash on those few hundred square yards of deadly battlefield, or passed aimlessly beyond the ridge and exploded harmlessly far over enemy territory. The Turks, being mostly under the farther lip of the small plateau, suffered little from the bombardment except on the knob which protruded into the line to Mac's left.

It was torn constantly by high explosive, and Turkish bodies were flung high in the air, in whole or in part. Equipment, earth and sandbags mixed with the sickly, murky green smoke which drifted in a choking cloud across Mac's line. Rapidly fresh Turks filled the places of their dead, and they in turn were blasted by the bombardment.

But many of the shells were falling short; or maybe they were not falling short, rather it was a position which should never have been bombarded in this fashion. The artillery was directed upon a hill high above it, lying between it and the breaking day. On its crest, separated by only a few yards, were both the defenders and the attackers. Few of the shells were likely to hit the enemy, for the majority must either spend themselves in the air beyond the crest or else fall among our own men on the crest itself; so they fell thickly along Mac's line, and thus to the danger of an enemy on three sides was added the tragedy of our own artillery on the fourth.

Helpless they were to shield themselves or to stop this mad destruction. They had red and yellow flags to mark their positions, and these they waved violently, but it could be of no avail in the dawn light, the dust and the smoke.

What telephone communication there was with the rear, Mac did not know; but whether there was any or whether it had been cut by the enemy, no sign came that the artillery knew where its shells were falling. One after another those shells burst with a yellow glare and a fountain of black smoke, sending men, some alive, and many dead, flying upwards; and when Mac could see again there would be a space in the line where one, two or more of his troop had taken the long trail. They rained faster, bursting incessantly on that narrow strip between them and the edge of the cliff, often falling behind and always odd ones and twos dropping into the trench itself. Mac felt sick with the fumes and the horror of it, and sometimes the blast of a shell sent him against the side of the trench.

The helplessness of the position appalled him. There were fewer and fewer of them left, and there was a growing gap in the line. Yet there was no means of stopping it; and he longed for the bombardment to cease. He sniped away at the Turks along the cliffs, and turned his attention at times to some who had been hunted from the knob by the shelling.

There were only three or four of them left in this corner and yet there was no slackening of that mad artillery fire. Then swiftly there was an awful lurid flash close in front of him, on the level ground almost in his face, and it seemed he had been hit across the head with a bar of wood, and he could not see. He pressed his hand to his face and sank slowly to the ground.

"Old Mac's a goner," he heard the voice of one of his mates say in those same affectionate, final tones which had followed the disappearance of comrade after comrade on the left.

"Poor old fellow," said another.

"No," muttered Mac. "By God though, I'm blind for life!" He felt the blood rushing down his face, and he knew it. He sat up, and no one said anything. He thought for a second or two and decided on a course of action. "Well, it's no longer any good staying here. I'm off." So, saying, he undid the buckles of his Webb equipment, and struggled out of all his gear, keeping only the case of his glasses, for he thought he might as well stick to them.

He remembered the way to the second line, and crawled along the shattered trench to the left, feeling his way past the legs of the one or two men who were left. They paid no attention to him, being too busy with the enemy to be concerned with other matters. He felt his way along on his hands and knees, down into holes, over dead bodies, avoiding wounded, across the open ground, until he came to where he thought the communication trench ought to be and turned to the left. There seemed to be little of it remaining. It had never been much of a thing, and was now blown about and full of wounded and dead. He was finding himself in difficulties about getting past some wounded men, when some one came out from the second line and led him in. There his captain took his hand and patted him on the back.

"I'm afraid I've lost my sight, sir," said Mac.

"I'm afraid so, old boy," replied he. "I'll send a chap back with you."

One of the boys took charge of him, and Mac stumbled off through the little piece of trench into the open, across which, from both sides, the bullets fled whistling and zipping. Jogging awkwardly short distances over the rough ground, then lying in hollows for brief rests, they covered at length that exposed slope of about one hundred and fifty yards which separated the trench from the shallow head of a ravine, wherein lay hundreds of wounded and dead. The trooper guided Mac carefully over a space where bodies lay thick, and made him lie down on a sloping clay bank, took his field dressing from his pocket and bandaged his head.

Mac lay there through the whole of that long terrible day, a day of strange unearthliness, when he seemed to float away into a weird dreamland and at times into nightmare, and yet it was not a day of unmixed suffering. The sun glared down pitilessly through the hot hours, the tormenting flies swarmed in their millions, the dead lay thick around, already blackening in the heat, the dying raved in delirium for water which never came, and the battle raged on with unceasing violence.

Lying uncomfortably on a slope, propped against a dead Turk, he scarcely seemed to feel the burning heat of the sun, the irritation of the flies, the torturing thirst nor the pain of his wound, for his spirit lay soothed in a strange restfulness, in the satisfaction of peace, in a manner like the weary wishing for nothing but sleep after a day of honest work. For Mac the fight was over; he had done what had been asked of him, and his spirit, serenely happy in this knowledge, seemed to rise above earthly discomfort and to concern itself little with the shattered state of his body, nor yet with the fact that he was far from out of the wood. Death was all around; and, had it come to him, he would have had no terror of it, but simply the resigned acceptance of a happy soul.

Early in the morning Mac had inquired whether he could not be taken on to the dressing-station, but learned that it was impossible as the enemy swept the country between with an impassable hail of bullets. The lower end of the ravine was in Turkish hands, elsewhere there were unscalable cliffs, and the only means of getting back was by crossing a ridge close under the enemy rifles. There was nothing for it but to await nightfall.

The ravine was full of wounded. The more lightly injured had drifted towards the bottom, but those who had not been able to walk lay crowded close in the shallow head near Mac. Most of them were already dead, for many had been wounded two nights previously, and few so seriously injured could stand a second day of such torment. Mac asked sometimes if there was water, but there was none. Occasionally he inquired how the battle was going, and if there were any men near to hear him, they replied only with unassuming grunts.

He sat up once for a change of position and moved away a little from the dead Turk, but the flying bullets sent him back. He may have been light-headed once or twice, but this he himself could not tell. Queerly enough, he troubled not at all about the form his wound had taken. Though he knew with absolute certainty that he would never see again, he was not worried by the horrors of a future world of darkness; and found himself in his vague wanderings of mind deeply pitying those round him, and his heart was full of grief at their sufferings.

Gradually a lessening of the heat told of coming evening. A little water arrived and was distributed in small potions. Mac was conscious that those who came periodically to the hollow to do for the wounded all that lay in their power were performing fine actions of self-sacrifice. It grew cool, and Mac stirred himself to expect aid from the rear; word had come, too, that a large Imperial force would be sent up at nightfall to relieve the tattered remnant of the garrison, who had dwindled to a desperate handful from attack after attack by the

112

enemy through all the long day, and who were almost light-headed from fatigue.

The hours still dragged on without anything happening, and Mac almost feared they had been forgotten. At last, shortly after he had heard a voice say it was eleven o'clock, some one came into the ravine, and inquired in the dark who were there. Few answered, for, it seemed to Mac, most of them were too far gone. All those who could look after themselves had long ago drifted farther down the ravine.

"Who are you?" sang out Mac.

"I'm an Auckland stretcher-bearer."

"Well, if you can show me the way, you can take me back. I can't see, but I can walk all right."

"I dunno how I'm goin' to get you out of there. There are too many wounded round you."

"Oh, if you show me where to tread, I'll be all right. You might as well take me back. I'm the only one here who can walk," said Mac appealingly.

After a little more persuasion, he picked his way over the bodies, and, Mac, swaying a little, stood up. He forgot to take the case of his glasses which he had been using as a pillow, though he had remembered afterwards that the glasses themselves were still on the parapet where he had been wounded. He picked his steps carefully over the prostrate forms, and then, grabbing the ambulance man firmly by the belt, stumbled after him up the slope. They toiled down the long ridge, falling frequently into hidden holes in the thick scrub; and all the time the rifles blazed along the ridges and the bullets zipped past them in the darkness. They reached the dressing-station, where, from the sounds which reached his ears, it seemed to him many men were lying, and a crowd passed constantly to and fro.

A medical officer took Mac in hand, dressed his wound as well as might be—for there was no water for such purposes—and gave him a drink. Though Mac protested he could quite well walk, the M.O. insisted on putting him on a stretcher, giving orders to the bearers to take him without delay to the hospital life-boats. And so, swaying precariously, he was taken away down the rough, steep slope, the bearers halting often to regain their breath. Then, taking not the slightest heed of his mild protests, they dumped him off the stretcher after they had gone about half a mile, spread a blanket over him and departed. He lay there peacefully for an hour or two, and then, becoming thoroughly fed up at this lack of progress and seeing no point in such delays, called out to someone he heard near him, to know what possibility there was of a further move.

"None, old boy," came the discouraging reply. "Stretchers are just about finish, and there are dozens of stretcher-cases lying everywhere. From the looks of things, you might be here for a day or two yet."

Mac thought for a minute or two and decided to take matters into his own hands. He heard someone passing along the path.

"Hullo you! Come over here," he called.

Someone approached.

"What's up, cobber?"

"If you're going to the rear you might as well take me along with you. I can walk all right. I only want a helping hand. What about it?"

"Well, I'm a Fifth Reinforcements just landed, an' I dunno where all my mates are gone."

"All right. You might as well come along with me." And so saying, Mac stood up, shed his blanket, and went off with the man who had lost himself.

It was broad daylight again, and the artillery activity was steadily increasing. They wandered down the dusty bottom of the ravine, Mac directing the way as best he could. At the bottom of the ravine, near a battery in furious action, they had to halt for some time owing to a congestion in the traffic through the big communication saps. Mac wanted to go along the top, but the other fellow refused flatly as there were too many bullets flying, and so they had to progress when opportunity offered through the hot dusty crowded saps.

They were close to the sea by No. 2 Outpost, but the hospital boats had ceased taking wounded off from there, owing to the heavy rifle fire. Mac decided to go on to Anzac without delay as, with weakness growing, he wished to keep going until he reached a hospital-ship. Dragging one foot after another, he plodded on through the interminable trenches, though swiftly his strength was going and he had to rest every twenty yards.

His companion, taking the wrong turning, led him over an unnecessary hill, which nearly exhausted his walking powers, but about nine o'clock they at length reached the cove and the clearing station. Mac's head was again dressed, he swallowed with the deepest joy many cups of tea, bid farewell to his escort, and lay down on some bales of hay to await the arrival of a hospital-ship, of which there were none at present off the landing.

CHAPTER 24
The End of Mac's Campaigning Days

About midday a hospital-ship anchored off the shore, and someone led him along the pier to a barge, from which he was transferred to a mine-sweeper, and at last was swung upwards by a crane on to the deck of the ship. He was almost the first on board. Kind hands and affectionate voices welcomed him, and tender hands led him along the deck to a surgery. The fresh cooling sea air had revived him, and here at last, with skilled hands and cool lotions easing his aching head, he felt supremely happy.

The blood and grime removed from his face, and a neat white bandage round his head, a sister took him in charge and guided him far down to a ward low in the ship. She gave him a comfortable bunk, and swiftly set about spring-cleaning him. She speedily unclothed him by running a pair of scissors along the sleeves and legs of his blood-clotted garments, giving him his precious bandages and identification disc wrapped up in a handkerchief; then sponged him all over in deliciously cool water, decked him in a shirt, and spread a sheet over him. Next came a large bowl of hot soup, which Mac lost no time in putting within his hungry frame, and finally a glass of port. The fine sister chatted away the while with pleasant little laughs and entertaining remembrances, as if she had not been working in those steamy holds for days and nights with scarce a rest. Many others were brought into the ward, and it was soon full of seriously wounded men, Imperial, Australian and New Zealand. M.O.'s and sisters worked incessantly at the heavy dressings.

The hours drifted slowly by, for though he had had no sleep for four days and nights, and little for several nights before that, he did not sleep, and the passage of time was marked only by the arrival of meals and the pleasant relief of fresh dressings. He was always hungry from long under-feeding, and relished everything which came his way. For him there was no difference between night and day, and he often lost count of time. There was only one sister in the ward, a splendid Queensland girl, who toiled for almost all of the twenty-four hours in the hot, steaming atmosphere, going steadily the round of the heavy dressings, starting again at the beginning as soon as she came to the last.

The ordinary routine work had to be left to the orderlies, and these men angered Mac so at times that he wished they might be lined up in a row and shot. Recruited, it seemed, from the lowest order of some community, they made use of this opportunity, when all senior ranks were too fully occupied with more immediate work of their own, to loaf, to rob the wounded sometimes, and to ignore many simple duties which for many men made all the difference between pain and comfort. Most of the wounded suffered from dysentery in a more or less acute form, and frequently seriously wounded men had to struggle out of bed to attend to the wants of those incapable of moving. Some exceptions there were, but the casual neglect in Mac's ward made him fume with anger.

But the sister and the *padre* were splendid people. The *padre* came to the ward to assist the sister with her dressings, and came to Mac to break gently the news that he would never see again. Mac had no illusions on this point, and laughed at the *padre* and his serious, funereal attitude till he resumed his normal cheery manner, when he and Mac soon discovered that they had many great friends in common in New Zealand, for the *padre* hailed from those parts too. The *padre* and sister became great friends of Mac, and in odd moments they sat on his bunk and yarned away with him, the *padre* about the Sounds' country which he and Mac knew so well, about what work Mac might do in future, and about all sorts of things, and with the sister he arranged some day to stay on the far back Queensland station.

The evening of the day he came on board they left Anzac and for some hours the engines rumbled away, when again there was silence. Mac was told they were at Mudros alongside the *Aquitania* putting all light and medium cases on board that vessel. Then for an indefinite space of time he again felt the vibration of the engines, and he thought they must be bound for Alexandria. When the vessel stopped, without having the vaguest notion how long she had been steaming, he took it for granted they were at Alexandria, and was rejoicing inwardly. He was deeply disappointed to hear they were again off Anzac.

During the day the Turks shelled the vessel, and turned machine-guns on her. The shells, which Mac could hear bursting as he lay in his bunk, did no damage, but the machine-gun fire caught one wounded man lying on deck, made several chips in the deck and holes through the operating theatre, narrowly missing a medical officer at work on a case and rattled against the steel sides. The ship moved out to a safer anchorage. Mac heard in later days that a destroyer had been carelessly firing from under the lee of the hospital ship. They took on board that day another thousand cases, again transferred the less seriously wounded to the *Aquitania*, and returned once more to Anzac. They left Anzac finally on Friday, called again at Mudros to discharge the light cases, and set a course for Alexandria, much to Mac's relief.

One day he was taken on a stretcher to the operating theatre, where he drifted strangely away from earthly things, and woke again in his bunk. Once he had a glorious sleep, after an injection of morphia, but usually he lay awake, tired and restless. There was no one to talk to, except on those rare but pleasant moments when the good *padre* and the ever-cheering sister found a few spare minutes. All those near him were badly wounded and far too ill to speak. Some died, and, wrapped in a blanket, disappeared from the ward to join the line of corpses on an upper deck, waiting the dawning hour and the parting words of the *padre* to plunge with firebars at their feet into the blue Mediterranean.

Of what had finally happened on those Gallipoli heights no one could say definitely, and there were disappointing and unsatisfactory rumours. About noon one day the vessel passed much wreckage of shattered boats, oars, sun helmets, lifebelts and so on, and cruised about for some time looking for survivors, but found none. It was the scene of the foundering a few hours earlier of the *Royal Edward* with many hundred fine fellows. The *padre* brought what news he could to Mac, and was seldom unaccompanied by something tempting in the way of sweets or fruit.

On Monday about the middle of the morning the vessel tied up at Alexandria. The heat was almost unbearable, for no breeze stirred in the hot confines of the dock to send a cooling breath into the stuffy depths of the ship. Mac had a wild longing to get off the ship, and he must have become light-headed. He had been told he would be sent ashore before evening, but it seemed to him hour after hour had passed and he knew it must be ten o'clock at night. He gave up hope, and said to the sister when she came near him that he supposed no one would be sent ashore now until morning.

"But it's only midday. You'll all go ashore this afternoon."

"Midday on Monday or Tuesday?" Mac inquired.

"Monday, of course, you silly old boy."

Days seemed to pass before the stretcher-bearers commenced removing the wounded from his ward, but it was only four in the afternoon when he was put on a stretcher, taken up in a lift and carried down the gangway across the pier to an ambulance. For those fifty yards through the fierce sun, an English woman walked beside him holding a parasol over his head, and he was deeply touched by so thoughtful a kindness. From what he had seen of the English ladies of Egypt during the terrible shortage of trained hospital workers, he knew that no words could describe the magnificence of their actions. The ambulance rattled away, and he heard again the many noises of an Egyptian street. It was a dreary journey of nearly an hour, for the springs of the car had long abandoned their functions, and the jolting over the cobbled roads was agony to his wounded head.

He was taken to the 17th General Hospital at Ramleh, and was placed on a low basket arrangement in a big marquee, with its sides rolled up so that the least hot of any stray breeze might find its way in. The floor was the desert sand. It was in these days that the shamefully inadequate preparations for the wounded were most felt, yet the sufferers themselves did not complain, and the hospital staffs and the civilian population of Egypt went to work in that scorching heat to make the best use of their strength and of the short supply of material available.

So the wounded, knowing that all there were doing their best uncomplainingly accepted going without dressings when they would have brought great relief; accepted bad food sometimes, the discomfort of the wicket beds in the stifling heat of the marquees; and, armed each with a fly whisk, they made the best of a bad job. The sisters were magnificent, and, indeed, everybody was. The lightly wounded, too, did all in their power for those who could not walk.

Several hours after Mac arrived, he was handed a bowl of rice mixed with condensed milk, and though it had been made some time, and had fermented, he was hungry and ate it eagerly. Then a sister dressed his wound, and soon the marquee was left to itself for the night. For the first time in several days, in spite of the fact that his head felt very bad, he went to sleep, and his waking was full of strange, unutterable horror. He found himself crawling with his hands and knees on the sand.

He was awake, but why was it he could not see? He crawled round and round, but could find nothing but sand, sand everywhere, nothing but sand. He felt terribly alone, and he could not recall the reason of it all, or why he could not see. He called out in his terror—again—and again—what, he did not know. Then an old sister seized him. "You poor old boy. What have you crawled out of the tent for?" And he remembered again where he was. She took him back to his bed, soothed him as a mother would calm a terrified child. Mac was trembling like a leaf.

Tuesday dragged wearily by. He was in low condition, and very, very tired and his head ached violently. Between the flies, the heat and the uncomfortable bed, it was not a happy home; but the kindness of the sisters and the other wounded men who came to him occasionally, went far towards making it all bearable. There were men worse than he in that marquee, men in agony and near to death, with torn, septic wounds, but sticking it out without a word.

Wednesday brought changes. The *padre* of the hospital ship had cabled to his father in London that he was all right, and what hospital he was going to; and now several people came to see him. Mac told them he would like to go home as soon as he could be sent, as there could be no more campaigning for him and the sooner, he was home the better. The M.O. said that a hospital-ship was leaving on the following day and that he would be sent by it. Mac was put in a ward that afternoon. He was brought some clothes for the morning, but, being fed up with bed, unknown to the sister, he donned them straight away and went and sat by the window. He felt very groggy, but getting up and about bucked him up tremendously.

Next morning, he took farewell of the sister, and, clad in a Tommy uniform built for some one many sizes smaller, a pair of heavy boots of huge calibre, and a Tommy cap perched on top of his bandages, he walked downstairs with an orderly. But out in the open the sun was too much for him and laid him low, when he was converted into a stretcher-case, and swung away on an ambulance much more comfortable than the one which brought him.

Again, he was carried across the sun-baked pier, sheltered from the sun and protected from the flies by one of those splendid Alexandrian women, and taken down into a comfortable bunk in the hospital-ship *Dongola*. Mac found in the adjutant of the ship a friend of bygone days, who placed him in a spare deck cabin, which he found not at all an unpleasant home for the next ten days.

He speedily gained strength at sea, and began to enjoy life a bit more. A fine Australian, who was but slightly wounded, took Mac under his wing, and with ceaseless care and affection walked with him on deck, and in a wonderfully unselfish way did many little things to make time pass quickly for him. A cheery Scottish sister poked her head in occasionally, and came in the evening to do his dressing. The orderly who brought Mac's meals, was an earnest, hardworking man, who had worked once with a missionary among the Eskimos, and who did the work of several lazy orderlies as well as his own. Late in the evening, as a special treat, he brought a gramophone up from below deck, stood it on a chair in the middle of the small cabin, directed the trumpet straight at Mac's head, and set in motion mournful hymn tunes.

It was tough going for his aching head; but the earnest orderly was so wrapped up in giving to him what he thought was great pleasure that he had not the heart to stop him. Mac would silence it for a time by encouraging dissertations on Eskimo life, or the future of the Gospel in India. An hour of the gramophone, and it would retire below to end its rasping for the day.

Twelve hot hours were passed in the Grand Harbour of Malta, while thousands of cackling fowls were lowered from the boat deck and sent ashore for men in hospital. The two following days Mac was almost entirely deserted, as a heavy sea sent most of the sisters, orderlies and patients to their bunks. The first night no one came to dress his head; but the second night a quaint rough stoker put in an appearance, and, chatting cheerfully the while, made his head more or less comfortable. No water came for washing, and on two rare occasions a fleeting orderly left a plate of some sort of food or other. He spent those two days in bed, and was thankful when they were over. From then onward the voyage went well, snoozing on deck in a chair, or walking up and down arm and arm with the Australian.

At length, in the keen air of an English autumn morning, Mac stood by the ship's rail as she moved quietly up Southampton Water, to berth in due course alongside a pier and a hospital train. Mac had dreamed that it might be so, though he scarcely dared to hope that it would come true; but the gangway was scarcely down before his father and his sister were on the deck and had him in their arms. In the middle of the afternoon the hospital train stopped at a Surrey station; and before very long he was being undressed, bathed and put to bed. Presently, the sister, the medical officer, his father and his sister withdrew quietly from the bright little room, saying that he must go to sleep after the excitements of the day. And to sleep Mac went, feeling more comfortable and happy than he had been for many a long day.

CHAPTER 25
Homeward

The tents sway and flap vigorously as gusts of wind tear through the camp, carrying clouds of sand across the island. Through the darkness comes the sound of the lashing of the date palms and the tamarisks as they swing to the gale. Within a straining, war-worn tent, lit by a flickering candle, stuck in a grease-streaked bottle, sit several mounted men of the old Brigade, their faces brown and weather-beaten from long campaigning in the Sinai Desert and amid Palestine hills.

The gear and stuff scattered casually about the tent tell it is the abode of an old hand of long service, who worries little about the frills of base and peace-time armies. And there, too, sprawled half-way across a camp bed is Mac. They yarn about old times, Gallipoli days and after, laughing often, though sometimes in affectionate, quieter tones they speak of a fallen comrade. It is midnight, the ill-used candle has not many minutes of life to run, and the desert wind bellows over the camp.

Three and a half years have passed since Mac found himself in the comfortable security of an English hospital—far from unpleasant years, during which the comradeship of his fellow-soldiers, and the kindness of many friends have fully made good the sight Mac lost on the summit of Chanak Bair. He has not lost touch with the men of the Expeditionary Force during their long weary years in France and Palestine, but has worked among them to the best of his limited powers. And now this stormy night in March 1919 finds him again with his old comrades of the Mounted Brigade, who, with a glorious campaign behind them, are resting for a while on an island on Lake Timsah till a transport at Suez is ready for them to embark.

Mac has visited old haunts and old friends in Egypt, and tomorrow he, too, goes on board his ship at Suez, bound for home. Again, there will be warm sleepy days in the Red Sea, with delicate sunsets and cool nights, a few sunny weeks in the tropics, some heavy weather, no doubt, south of Australia, and then New Zealand.

Nearly five years of war, strange adventures and experiences of the wider world have brought changes in the lives of those whose fate was not to fall in the field, and have left them a little sadder and, maybe, a little wiser. Mac's life must be vastly changed from the old one, and for him there will be no more work with his dogs among the sheep and cattle, and no more of many of the old things. But he has no regrets. Least of all does he regret the day which first found him a trooper of the Mounted Rifles. Others may forget the men who went away, many never to return; but deep in the hearts of their comrades will be fully valued those years of campaigning, when they knew the unselfish sacrifices of comradeship, the careless courage, the humour, and the affection of man.

Through these years Mac often thought of that wild winter day in the bush when he and Charley, looking at the old Boer War pictures, had resented the fact that they had been too young to join in it, and that there was no, war for them to go to. Within a year Charley had been killed, wounded three times in an attack at Cape Helles; and three months later Mac himself had been incapacitated for life. Their longing for war had been fulfilled with a vengeance. True, war had brought them no good; but it had had many grand moments, power to strengthen character and inspiration towards great thought, art and unselfishness. Tragedy, crime and disease had also followed in its train, though, for his part, Mac thought that some good must come of it all.

www.ingramcontent.com/pod-product-compliance
Lightning Source LLC
Chambersburg PA
CBHW031900090426
42741CB00005B/580